T0183867

Communications in Computer and Information Science   589

Commenced Publication in 2007
Founding and Former Series Editors:
Alfredo Cuzzocrea, Dominik Ślęzak, and Xiaokang Yang

More information about this series at http://www.springer.com/series/7899

Kristin Haltinner · Dilshani Sarathchandra
Jim Alves-Foss · Kevin Chang
Daniel Conte de Leon · Jia Song (Eds.)

Cyber Security

Second International Symposium, CSS 2015
Coeur d'Alene, ID, USA, April 7–8, 2015
Revised Selected Papers

 Springer

Editors

Kristin Haltinner
University of Idaho
Moscow, ID
USA

Kevin Chang
University of Idaho
Moscow, ID
USA

Dilshani Sarathchandra
University of Idaho
Moscow, ID
USA

Daniel Conte de Leon
University of Idaho
Moscow, ID
USA

Jim Alves-Foss
University of Idaho
Moscow, ID
USA

Jia Song
University of Idaho
Moscow, ID
USA

ISSN 1865-0929   ISSN 1865-0937   (electronic)
Communications in Computer and Information Science
ISBN 978-3-319-28312-8   ISBN 978-3-319-28313-5   (eBook)
DOI 10.1007/978-3-319-28313-5

Library of Congress Control Number: 2015958547

Printed on acid-free paper

This Springer imprint is published by SpringerNature
The registered company is Springer International Publishing AG Switzerland

Preface

The 2015 Cybersecurity Symposium: Your Security, Your Future was the second in a series of conferences hosted by the Center for Secure and Dependable Systems (CSDS). The symposium offered a key opportunity for academic researchers and system stakeholders from industry and government organizations to meet and discuss state-of-the-art and state-of-the-practice techniques and processes related to cybersecurity. The objective of the symposium was to provide a platform for stakeholders to collaborate and exchange ideas and processes to help improve the security of today's critical systems. The 2015 Cybersecurity Symposium was partially funded by the State of Idaho and CSDS.

Since its inception in 2014, the symposium has attracted national and international stakeholders, including engineers, practitioners, researchers, and learners from industry, government, and academia. The 2015 conference brought together approximately 50 attendees from diverse locations such as the US East and West Coast and Europe. Hence, the opportunities created by this symposium to bring world-class knowledge and state and nationwide interest to the ongoing efforts in cybersecurity by the University of Idaho and the State of Idaho are significant.

The 2015 conference received 20 extended abstracts and 11 full-paper submissions. The peer-review process for extended abstracts and research papers included two stages. In the first stage, all potential participants submitted extended abstracts. These abstracts were reviewed by the Organizing Committee. Authors of extended abstracts deemed suitable for the conference goals were invited to present their research at the symposium and to submit full papers for consideration for the conference proceedings. In the second stage, full-paper submissions went through a series of anonymous peer-reviews. The resulting detailed reviews were given to all draft authors. Decisions about final paper acceptance were reviewed and approved by the Organizing Committee. The committee accepted nine papers to be included in the 2015 proceedings.

The collection of papers in these proceedings reflect four areas of scholarly work: (1) permissions and trust evaluation, implementation, and management; (2) cloud and device security and privacy; (3) social implications of networked and mobile applications, and (4) system and process assessments for improved cybersecurity. These areas demonstrate a maturity in the fields of cybersecurity and privacy by providing novel examples of secure computer systems and associated theoretical advances.

The results and case studies presented in these proceedings capture the scope of current knowledge as well as potential future applications. Previous books on cybersecurity and privacy have been largely divided by discipline. Industry has discovered the limitations to current security measures, social scientists have investigated public attitudes and behavior toward privacy and security, engineers have investigated risks of cybersecurity breaches in critical infrastructures, and computer scientists have explored practical measures that can be taken to maximize online security while maintaining some level of privacy for users. Until recently, these fields have operated in a non-collaborative fashion resulting in a limited understanding of how technology development and adoption are affected by broader societal needs.

The present proceeding are an attempt at merging the knowledge and strengths of a number of different fields. Because we have included scholarly and professional work from the social sciences, computer science, engineering, and infrastructure, this volume provides a comprehensive and practical information source for graduate students, faculty, industry, governmental organizations, and other stakeholders who are interested cybersecurity and privacy.

The careful selection and organization of the papers in this volume extends the fields of cybersecurity and privacy in several important ways. The Cybersecurity Symposium and resulting conference proceedings:

- Provide a platform for industry and academia to merge their knowledge and experience
- Present a clear analysis of the challenges faced by the public and private sector while simultaneously connecting these issues with current, cutting-edge, computer science research
- Bring human factors into the analysis of cybersecurity and privacy concerns
- Present an avenue for social scientists and computer scientists to deepen their understanding of security needs and privacy demands
- Include an analysis of the problems and opportunities in cybersecurity as it applies to critical infrastructures
- Present an analysis of the economic impacts of cybersecurity

We look forward to this publication bridging cybersecurity advances in academia, industry, and governmental organizations and providing a foundation to future developments in the fields of cybersecurity and privacy.

October 2015

Kristin Haltinner
Dilshani Sarathchandra
Jim Alves-Foss
Kevin Chang
Daniel Conte de Leon
Jia Song

Organization

The 2015 Cybersecurity Symposium was organized by the Center for Secure and Dependable Systems of the University of Idaho. The center is partly sponsored by the Idaho Global Entrepreneurial Mission. The conference was held at the Coeur d'Alene Resort.

Programme Committee and Local Organizing Committee

Jim Alves-Foss	University of Idaho, Secure and Dependable Systems, USA
Kevin Chang	University of Idaho, Department of Civil Engineering, USA
Daniel Conte de Leon	University of Idaho, Secure and Dependable Systems, USA
Arvilla Daffin	University of Idaho, Secure and Dependable Systems, USA
Kristin Haltinner	University of Idaho, Department of Sociology and Anthropology, USA
Jia Song	University of Idaho, Secure and Dependable Systems, USA

Contents

Permissions and Trust Evaluation, Implementation, and Management

Expanding RTEMS to a Multiuser System by Using Security Tags

Jia Song$^{(\boxtimes)}$ and Jim Alves-Foss

University of Idaho, Moscow, ID 83844, USA
{jsong,jimaf}@uidaho.edu

Abstract. This paper discusses a research project that develops enhanced security protections for operating systems running on security enhanced microprocessors. Security tagging schemes are promising mechanisms for enhancing the security of computer systems. The idea of tagging schemes is to attach metadata tags to memory and registers to carry information about the data being tagged. This paper summarizes the features of these new microprocessors and discusses the use of these features in the design of enhanced operating system security for an exemplary real time operating system.

1 Security Tagging Schemes

Computers play an increasingly important role in modern life and it is now widely recognized that people need to pay more attention to computer security issues. Over the years, researchers and developers have devised various techniques including encryption, firewalls, and virus scanners to provide secure computing environments. The idea of enhancing these mechanisms by using hardware to provide security features for operating systems and user applications is not new. Decades ago researchers proposed techniques to add security labels (tags) at the hardware level to help with the enforcement of system security properties [1,3]. Unfortunately, these techniques required more computing resources and memory than was feasible at the time. As hardware speeds have improved, the idea of security tagging has resurfaced as a promising mechanism for enhancing security.

Security tagging schemes attach labels to memory and/or registers to carry information about data during program execution. These labels are also called tags. They have been used by researchers to ensure that the semantics of computations are correctly implemented; to isolate code and data, users and system; and to enforce security policies at the hardware level. The implementation of tagging in hardware provides developers with enhanced security mechanisms without a penalty on performance, as compared to traditional microprocessors. Therefore, tagging schemes are seen as promising mechanisms to help processors and OSs (Operating Systems) implement security properly.

Security tagging schemes are known as promising mechanisms for enhancing the security of computer systems. Security tagging was first designed and implemented to protect against some low-level attacks, such as buffer overflow and

© Springer International Publishing Switzerland 2016
K. Haltinner et al. (Eds.): CSS 2015, CCIS 589, pp. 3–18, 2016.
DOI: 10.1007/978-3-319-28313-5_1

format string attacks [6,7,12,14]. Recently, security tagging schemes have been improved to prevent high-level attacks, which include SQL (Structured Query Language) injection and cross-site scripting [2,4]. Tags are also implemented in some specific architectures to support memory access control [8,9,13,15]. The details of the comparison of these tagging schemes can be found in another paper of the authors [11].

As part of the University of Idaho's (UI) UITags research project, a tagging scheme has been developed to secure RTEMS (Real-Time Executive for Multi-processor Systems). In the UI tagging scheme, a 32-bit tag is associated with every 32-bit memory and registers. The tag consists of three fields: Owner field, Code-space field and Control-bits field. These fields provide information about who owns the data, who can manipulate the data and other information for further control the tagged data. During system execution, tags are checked and propagated appropriately. Different from traditional operating systems, RTEMS can be decomposed into many smaller components. Each component provides a set of unique services to support the running of the system. Based on the functionality and importance of the component, tags are associated with the code to represent security levels. Furthermore, tagging rules were implemented to help control the information flows in the RTEMS.

The original version of RTEMS implements a single-user multi-threaded model of execution. To expand it to a multiuser system, the concepts of "superuser" and "non-privileged user" were used. A superuser is a user who has authority to create, delete, and control non-privileged users. Non-privileged users are isolated from each other and can only control themselves, but have no abilities to create, delete or control other users. By assigning different user tags to the data/code of the system and user application, the data and code can be seen as belonging to a specific user. Based on the tag, the system knows the specific permissions that the code/data have, and therefore protects its resources from being accessed by non-authority users. We expanded RTEMS from a single user system to multiuser system, implementing a user manager module to handle the multiuser issues. This paper briefly reviews the overall UI security tagging scheme, provides details of the implementation of tags for multiple users and how the system code was changed to support the advanced security tagging scheme for multiuser RTEMS system. Future work is also proposed at the end of the paper.

2   RTEMS

RTEMS [5] consists of a super core (SCORE) and 18 managers. The 18 managers provide different services and the SCORE provides kernel functions that support the managers. After examining the code of RTEMS, we found that it has very little security built in. Therefore, the UI tagging scheme has been developed with the purpose to secure the RTEMS.

2.1   RTEMS Architecture

The original 18 managers of RTEMS provide services to user code in support of concepts such as tasks, memory, timers, and communications. Each manager provides a well-defined set of services through directives that take the place of traditional system calls. Each manager also has internal functions that it uses to support implementation, some of these are private to the specific manager, and some are intended to be used by other managers. In either case, these manager internal functions are not intended to be used by user code.

In addition to each manager, RTEMS has a set of modules that make up the SCORE subsystem. The SCORE provides services for all managers, and all managers interact with the SCORE via directives. Some major SCORE modules are: object, thread, chain, interrupt service routine (ISR), error handler, heap and protected heap, workspace, initialization, message, time, watch dog, and user extension. These modules are key to the internal working of RTEMS, but are not intended for use by user code.

Conceptually the APIs are meant to be externally accessible, internally restricted to other RTEMS modules or internal to specific modules. However, RTEMS currently does not restrict access to any of these functions or their private data structures. The following sections outline the major security concerns that need to be addressed to secure RTEMS.

2.2 Security Concerns in RTEMS

The examination of RTEMS's source code reveals several major security concerns.

No Separation Between User and System. In RTEMS, there is no separation between user resources and system resources. In traditional operating systems, the system has ultimate privileges while the user has limited privileges. In RTEMS, both the user and system have ultimate privileges. Currently user code can use all of the SCORE code, internal functions, and directives. This means that the user can do everything that the RTEMS system can. For example, the user has privileges to change the system configuration, delete system tasks, etc. This is a design decision since RTEMS is intended for embedded systems and is built for high performance. Unfortunately, this limits the use of RTEMS in secure environments or from safely running untrusted code.

System has no Protection from Users. RTEMS has no protection from users and no concept of multiple users. Take the directive, `rtems_task_delete`, as an example. There is no check of the identity of the caller of this directive. This means that other system managers can use this directive, other system code can use it, and even users can delete any task by calling this directive. There is no restriction on who can delete which task, which means that users could even delete system threads.

No Separation of RTEMS Code. There is no isolation among RTEMS managers, directives and SCORE. In RTEMS, SCORE works as the micro kernel of the system. If the SCORE code is misused by a user or attacked by a malicious user, critical security problems may occur. Therefore it is important that SCORE code be separated from other system code and user code.

RTEMS has 18 managers and each manager has its own functionality. Each manager has specific directives that support the manager. RTEMS has internal functions that help RTEMS managers function correctly, inline routines that speed up the running of RTEMS, and library functions supporting some of the functionalities. In the current version of RTEMS, every directive of a RTEMS module can call any function, including internal functions of other RTEMS modules. This may cause security problems if any application in user code is modified by an attacker, because the attacked code can use any other RTEMS code that the attacker wants. With a Security Tagged Architecture (STA), mechanisms can be implemented in RTEMS to prevent unintended or malicious usage of manager and SCORE code.

No Separation of Different Users. Although RTEMS has a single user multi-threaded model of execution, it can be expanded to be a multiuser system. To be extended to a multiuser system, the system must have a method to identify the owner of user data and keep it separated from other users' data. However, RTEMS cannot tell which user is the owner of specific user data. For a thread, it might be a thread generated by user 1, a thread generated by user 2, or a system thread. Since the owner of the thread is unknown, who has the permission to change or delete it can not be specified. Currently RTEMS is a single user system that contains no rules to specify who can do what. This becomes a problem when RTEMS is extended to allow more than one user.

3   UI Security Tagging Scheme

3.1   Tag Format and Its Composition

As shown in Fig. 1, the tag is a 32-bit tag which consists of three fields: Owner, Code-space, and Control-bits. The tag can be written as ($\langle$Owner$\rangle$, $\langle$Code $-$ space$\rangle$, $\langle$Control $-$ bits$\rangle$). In a tag, each of the Owner and Code-space fields is represented with 12 bits, with the remaining 8 bits for the Control-bits.

Owner Field. In the implemented tagging scheme, the first field, the Owner field, helps separate system code/data and user code/data. It indicates the identity of the owner of the data or code. The values of the Owner field can be classified into six major classes: SCORE internal, SCORE, Manager internal, Manager, Startup and User. The SCORE internal class can be further divided into three groups: SCORE internal init, SCORE internal private and SCORE internal. The Manager internal class is also broken into three groups: Manager internal init, Manager internal private and Manager internal.

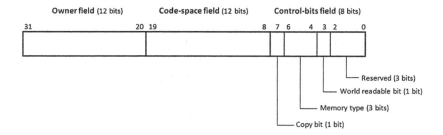

Fig. 1. Tag format

By using the Owner field, the owner of data or code can be easily identified. For example, the first field in the tag (object, ⟨Code − space⟩, ⟨Control − bits⟩) indicates that the data or code associated with this tag is object code or object data; where object is one of the SCORE modules. A tag (task manager, ⟨Code − space⟩, ⟨Control − bits⟩) shows that the data or code is owned by the task manager. In the remaining sections, ⟨SCORE⟩ in the tag means this field could be one of the possible values in the SCORE class, and the same holds for the Startup class, SCORE internal class, Manager class, Manager internal class and User class. Although RTEMS currently only supports a single user, it is expanded to a multiuser system as part of this paper (see Sect. 4). Therefore, multiple users are listed in the possible values of the User class. Having different users for the Owner field ensures that a user can only access its own data and code, but not other users' resources.

Code-Space Field. The second field of the tag is the Code-space field. This field shows which code space should manage the data or code. In addition to this, the Code-space field is also critical for information flow control and memory access control. The possible values of the Code-space field are the same as the Owner field. The Code-space can be ⟨User⟩, ⟨Manager⟩, ⟨Manager internal⟩, ⟨SCORE⟩, ⟨SCORE internal⟩ and ⟨Startup⟩. For example, the tag (User1, Manager1, ⟨Control − bits⟩) means the data are created in manager1's code for user1. Manager1 is used as a place holder for a specific manager name, such as task manager, partition manager, etc.

Code-space is used to show the class of the code or data and helps control function calls. Users in the system should only use the manager directives, and not directly use SCORE, SCORE internal, and Manager internal functions. Therefore, firstly, Code-space is used to indicate which class the code belongs to, and then rules can be provided to control which classes of code can use which other classes of code.

Control-Bits Field. The Control-bits field is used for further control. It starts with a single copy bit (bit 7) which indicates whether a return value has been modified. The copy bit allows user code to have a copy of a trusted data value

Table 1. Possible values of the memory type

Memory type	Read or read/write
Data memory (x00)	000 read-only
	100 - read/write
Stack memory (x01)	001 read-only
	101 - read/write
Code memory (executable) not entry point (x10)	010 read-only
	110 - read/write
Code memory (executable) entry point (x11)	011 read-only
	111 - read/write

(i.e., a task ID) as long as it is not changed. The notation $\overline{cp}$ means the copy bit is not set while cp indicates the copy bit is set. The return value to a user will be tagged with the security class of the directive and will have the copy bit set. If the copy bit remains set, this means that the user has not made any change to the value. If the copy bit is not set, the data is treated as modified data and will not be accepted when used as a parameter to a directive. This allows user programs to store copies of system IDs and handles while maintaining security of the values. For example, if user1 uses directive code from the task manager to get a tag identifier, the directive returns an identifier tagged (user1, task manager, cp). If the user modifies this returned ID, the tag will be changed to (user1, user1, $\overline{cp}$) to indicate this ID has been changed; and the OS will no longer trust the ID. This allows the system to trust IDs that come from users without having to keep an internal table of indirect identifiers or separate tables for each user, and thereby improve performance and simplify system code.

Three of the control bits (bits 6 to 4) are allocated for memory type. To further protect data in memory, memory is divided into three classes: stack memory, code memory, and data memory. These three bits specify the memory type, such as readable, writable, read-only, executable, entry point, data memory, and stack memory.

- **Stack Memory.** Stack memory is readable and writable, and is treated using register expression rules for stores, instead of assignment rules.
- **Code Memory.** Code memory stores the executable and readable code. The "entry point" of a function has a special tag with it to indicate the correct starting address for executing a function.
- **Data Memory.** All other memory is data memory which is readable and writable, and it is treated using assignment rules.

The possible values of the memory type are shown in Table 1.

A world-readable bit (bit 3) is used to indicate that the tagged data can be read by all entities; It can be used when the system (higher level) wants to give the user (lower level) permission to access some data, such as configuration data.

The other 3 bits (bits 2 to 0) are reserved for future use.

3.2   Tag Representation

In a tag, each of the Owner and Code-space fields is represented with 12 bits, with the remaining 8 bits for the Control-bits. For Owner field and Code-space field, the higher 4 of the 12 bits are used to indicate if the tagged data or code is a system resource or not. If the higher 4 bits are 1111, this means that the tagged data or code is from the system, otherwise it is from users. For system code (tags that start with 1111), the lower eight bits are used to divide the code into smaller classes. Among the 8 lower bits, the higher 3 bits indicate the level of the class, and the lower 5 bits represent which component. For example, the level of class includes SCORE internal class, SCORE private internal class, SCORE internal init class, SCORE external class, manager internal class, manager private internal class, manager internal init class, manager external class. The 5 bits which represent the component of the RTEMS can be a specific manager or SCORE, such as task manager, partition manager, SCORE thread, SCORE interrupt service routine and etc.

For the user code and data, all of 12 bits of the Owner field or Code-space field are used to represent a user. When expanding the system to a multiuser system, the 12 bits are further divided to support multiple users (see Sect. 4).

3.3   Lattice

Since the Owner field and Code-space field are used to define the security class of the data, the ideas similar to those of the Data Mark Machine (DMM) [3] can be implemented to control the information flows within RTEMS. The solution is a bit different from DMM since a hierarchy is defined for confidentiality and integrity controls, and it is not for traditional multi-level security. However, accesses still can be controlled to prevent "lower-level" entities from unauthorized access to higher level entities.

The lattice model of information flow deals with channels of information flow and policies. For the lattice model of information flow, there exists a lattice with a finite set of security classes and a partial ordering between the classes. The nodes of the lattice represent the individual security classes. The notation $\leq$ denotes the partial ordering relation between two classes of information. For example, $A \leq B$ means class A is at a lower or equal level than class B. The notation $\oplus$ denotes the least upper bound (LUB) operation.

In a lattice, there exists a unique class $C = A \oplus B$ such that:

$A \leq C$ and $B \leq C$, and
$A \leq D$ and $B \leq D$ implies $C \leq D$ for all D in the lattice.

The security class of an entity in the model, a, will be denoted as $\underline{a}$, and it can be written as $\underline{a} = (\texttt{Owner(a)}, \texttt{Code} - \texttt{space(a)})$. The Control-bits are ignored in this discussion since they are used separately from the lattice-based controls and formulas. $\texttt{Owner(a)}$ refers to just the Owner field of a's tag, $\texttt{Code-space(a)}$ refers to the Code-space field of the tag of a.

The definition of the LUB, $\oplus$, of the security classes of two tags is:

If $\underline{a}$ = (Owner(a), Code-space(a)), and $\underline{b}$ = (Owner(b), Code-space(b)),
then $\underline{a} \oplus \underline{b}$ = (Owner(a) $\oplus$ Owner(b), Code $-$ space(a) $\oplus$ Code $-$ space(b)).

The definition of the equality of the security classes of two tags is:

If $\underline{a}$ = (Owner(a), Code-space(a)), and $\underline{b}$ = (Owner(b), Code-space(b)),
then if Owner(a) = Owner(b) and Code $-$ space(a) = Code $-$ space(b), then
the security class of a and b are the same.

The definition of the domination of the security classes of two tags is:

If $\underline{a}$ = (Owner(a), Code-space(a)), and $\underline{b}$ = (Owner(b), Code-space(b)),
then if Owner(a) $\subseteq$ Owner(b) and Code $-$ space(a) $\subseteq$ Code $-$ space(b), then
the security class of a dominates the security class of b.

The similar rules for $\leq$, $<$, $\geq$ and $>$ operations can be defined similarly and
are not shown here.

3.4 Tagging Rules for the Basic Values in C

At the start of the system, and as each subroutine is called, data and code tags
are initialized with the correct security classification and memory types. This
section discusses how those classifications can be used, in the context of the C
programming language, to define tagging rules needed to satisfy the security
concerns based on the partial ordering and lattice concepts.

This section introduces the basic concepts of using tags at the C language
level. The full details can be found in the corresponding literature [10].

- During execution of a program, the tag of the current running thread is the
  same as the security class of the program counter, denoted as $\underline{PC}$.
- The tag of the variable a is the tag of the memory location of a and its security
  class is denoted $\underline{a}$.
- The tag of a literal, or constant, n, is the same as the tag of the PC. This is
  because the use of the literal is controlled by the current thread.
- The security class of the tag of an array item, a[i] is the least upper bound
  of the security class of the index to the array and the security class of the
  memory location referenced by the array: $\underline{a[i]} = \underline{i} \oplus [[a + i]]$ where [[a+i]]
  denotes the memory address referenced by a[i]. In cases where the copy bit
  of the memory location is set, the tag of that memory location is used instead
  of the LUB.
- The tag of a value referenced by a pointer, *p or structure p->fld or p.fld
  is the tag of the memory location referenced. For example, $\underline{*p} = [[p]]$ where
  [[p]] denotes the memory address referenced by the pointer p.
- All code will be tagged as read-only, executable memory, and all entry points
  to functions will be tagged as function entry points (to avoid problems with
  the misuse of function pointers).
- All data memory will be tagged as read-write data memory.

3.5   Tag Manager and Tag Engine

To support the UI tagging scheme, a tag manager has been added to RTEMS to allow the OS to handle the tagging issue, for example checking if the copy bit is set or not in some specific functions and take or release the ownership of some data. These tag checking and propagation can not be done at the hardware level easily. Some tagging functions have been inserted into special RTEMS functions to satisfy special requirements of the tagging scheme, such as setting the copy bit of the ID's tag that is going to be returned from some RTEMS functions.

The tag engine has been implemented at the hardware level to support the tagging scheme. The tag engine can be turned on and off to test the whole tagging system. Tag engine rules have been applied to different instructions. Therefore when executing an instruction, the tag engine rules for the specific instruction will be checked to ensure the instruction is allowed to be executed based on the tagging rules. If that is not the case, the tag engine will generate an error message and terminate the program.

4   Security Tagging Scheme for Multiuser System

To expand RTEMS to support multiple users, a new "user" construct has been added to RTEMS, similar to the task construct. To manage the users, the concepts of "superuser" and "non-privileged user" have been defined. All control is managed through a new user manager.

4.1   Implementation of the Multiple User System

Before our work, RTEMS implemented a single-user multi-threaded model of execution. To expand it to a multiuser system, the concepts of "non-privileged user" and "superuser" have to be supported. A superuser is a user who has authority to create, delete, and control non-privileged users. Non-privileged users are isolated from each other and can only control themselves, but have no abilities to create, delete or control other users.

The new RTEMS user model allows for 117 non-privileged user IDs and one superuser. Each user can have up to 32 separated task IDs. To have more control over users and their tasks, a set of task IDs is provided to each user. This allows additional secure isolation between the tasks within a single user. To implement this, the user levels' Owner field of the tag is divided into two parts – users and tasks. The higher 7 bits among the 12 bits are used to represent separate user IDs and the lower 5 bits are used to indicate task IDs for those users. For example, the 12 bits for the superuser are 1110 110 XXXXX, where the 1110 110 indicates superuser ID and the XXXXX represents task IDs. Since only 7 bits are used to represent different users, this limits the number of users in the system to be user1 to user117 (0000 001 XXXXX to 1110 101 XXXXX), recalling that 1111 XXX XXXXX is reserved for RTEMS code. Including the superuser, there are 118 possible users in the system. For an embedded system, 118 users

Table 2. New bit representation for Owner field of USER and LOW levels

USER	1110 111 11111
Superuser	1110 110 XXXXX
user117	1110 101 XXXXX
...	...
user2	0000 010 XXXXX
user1	0000 001 XXXXX
LOW	0000 000 00000

each with 32 possible subtasks should be sufficient. The implementation of 118 users does not influence the levels above the general user (USER) level, because separate controls are made for users and their tasks. The new bit representation for Owner field of tags are shown in Table 2.

4.2   User Manager

To change RTEMS to a multiuser system, system code needs to be modified to support multiple users. This includes adding a user manager to RTEMS to handle the superuser and its abilities to create, delete and control non-privileged users and corresponding changes to the tag manager. In addition, the simulator needed modification of the tag engine code to support the user hierarchy rules.

The user manager is supported by several user manager directives, such as rtems_user_create directive, rtems_user_manager_initialization directive and rtems_user_delete directive, etc.

Take the rtems_user_create directive as an example, this directive checks the caller of the directive and creates a non-privileged user. It first checks that the calling user is the superuser, because only the superuser is authorized to create, control and delete the non-privileged users. If this is the case, rtems_user_allocate gets the next available user id, starting at 1, and updates its internal data structures. After getting the user number, the get_user_tag is called to get a specific tag associated with the task_ids and task_names for that user. For example, if user number is 1, then a tag (USER1, USER1, true | READWRITE | DATA_MEMORY | WORLD_NOT_READABLE) is returned. If user number is 2, the function get_user_tag will return a tag, (USER2, USER2, true | READWRITE | DATA_MEMORY | WORLD_NOT_READABLE). Further in the function, _rtems_tag_word is used to tag the task_ids and task_names. (Although tags are associated with pointers, they are actually being attached to the memory location referenced by the pointer.)

In multiuser RTEMS, a user program is assigned a primary application with task id 0. This is the first application to execute for the user. The primary application for a user first declares an array of task_id and another array of task_name. When creating a task, the user application passes two pointers to the rtems_task_create directive which point to the task_id and task_name. Then the directive creates the task for the user application and returns a system-wide unique `task_id` back. By using the system `task_id`, the user application is able to start, suspend, resume, or delete the task.

4.3 Multiuser Example

The multiuser example starts from an `Init` function. The `Init` function first uses the `rtems_user_create` function twice to create two non-privileged users. In this example the PC's tag is manually set to the SUPERUSER. Normally this will happen in the kernel prior to calling `Init`. The result of calling the `rtems_user_create` function is shown in Fig. 2. The `Task_id[1]` to `Task_id[4]` are tagged with user1's tag, and `Task_id[5]` to `Task_id[7]` are tagged with user2's tag.

Then the user application sends `Task_id[1]` to `Task_id[4]` to the directive, `rtems_task_create`, to create four new tasks separately. The directive then creates four tasks and stores the RTEMS task ids into the `Task_id[1]` to `Task_id[4]` respectively. The copy bit of the tags associated with `Task_id[1]` to `Task_id[4]` will be set. Similarly, another three tasks will be created by user2 for `Task_id[5]` to `Task_id[7]`.

The four tasks created for user1 are different from the three tasks for user2. User1's tasks keep printing out the time every five seconds. After starting user2's tasks, the tasks are suspended for 15 s and then wake up to attempt to delete user1's tasks.

The seven tasks run concurrently. Figure 3 shows output of the tasks running without the tag engine turned on. At the first 15 s, tasks 1 to 4 are running and printing time information every five seconds. After 15 s, task 5 starts to delete task 1, task 6 deletes task 3 and task 7 deletes task 4. After successful deletion of these tasks, only task 2 is still alive and running.

The output of running the seven tasks is displayed in Fig. 4. With tag engine turned on, when user2's task (task 5) wants to delete user1's task (task 1), the tag engine generates an exception, prints an error message and stops the system.

```
***********This is INIT (SUPERUSER) function!!***********
*** SAMPLE SINGLE PROCESSOR MULTIUSER APPLICATION ***
Creating and starting an application task

user1 created!!
id_ptr tag: <User 1,User 1,CP=true,WorldReadable=false,Read-Write Data Memory>
Task_id[ 1 ] tag: <User 1,User 1,CP=true,WorldReadable=false,Read-Write Data Memory>
Task_id[ 2 ] tag: <User 1,User 1,CP=true,WorldReadable=false,Read-Write Data Memory>
Task_id[ 3 ] tag: <User 1,User 1,CP=true,WorldReadable=false,Read-Write Data Memory>
Task_id[ 4 ] tag: <User 1,User 1,CP=true,WorldReadable=false,Read-Write Data Memory>

user2 created!!
id_ptr2 tag: <User 2,User 2,CP=true,WorldReadable=false,Read-Write Data Memory>
Task_id[ 5 ] tag: <User 2,User 2,CP=true,WorldReadable=false,Read-Write Data Memory>
Task_id[ 6 ] tag: <User 2,User 2,CP=true,WorldReadable=false,Read-Write Data Memory>
Task_id[ 7 ] tag: <User 2,User 2,CP=true,WorldReadable=false,Read-Write Data Memory>

The current running task is 0
```

Fig. 2. Result of a successful call of user create function

```
^^^^^^IN app task, the task_index2 = 1
 - rtems_clock_get_tod - 05:00:00   12/31/1988
^^^^^^IN app task, the task_index2 = 2
 - rtems_clock_get_tod - 05:00:00   12/31/1988
^^^^^^IN app task, the task_index2 = 3
 - rtems_clock_get_tod - 05:00:00   12/31/1988
^^^^^^IN app task, the task_index2 = 4
 - rtems_clock_get_tod - 05:00:00   12/31/1988
^^^^^^IN app task, the task_index2 = 1
 - rtems_clock_get_tod - 05:00:05   12/31/1988
^^^^^^IN app task, the task_index2 = 2
 - rtems_clock_get_tod - 05:00:05   12/31/1988
^^^^^^IN app task, the task_index2 = 3
 - rtems_clock_get_tod - 05:00:05   12/31/1988
^^^^^^IN app task, the task_index2 = 4
 - rtems_clock_get_tod - 05:00:05   12/31/1988
^^^^^^IN app task, the task_index2 = 1
 - rtems_clock_get_tod - 05:00:10   12/31/1988
^^^^^^IN app task, the task_index2 = 2
 - rtems_clock_get_tod - 05:00:10   12/31/1988
^^^^^^IN app task, the task_index2 = 3
 - rtems_clock_get_tod - 05:00:10   12/31/1988
^^^^^^IN app task, the task_index2 = 4
 - rtems_clock_get_tod - 05:00:10   12/31/1988
^^^^^^IN app task, the task_index2 = 1
 - rtems_clock_get_tod - 05:00:15   12/31/1988

******IN tick task, the task_index2 = 5
 - ***rtems_clock_get_tod - 05:00:00   12/31/1988
task-5 delete task 1!
^^^^^^IN app task, the task_index2 = 2
 - rtems_clock_get_tod - 05:00:15   12/31/1988

******IN tick task, the task_index2 = 6
 - ***rtems_clock_get_tod - 05:00:00   12/31/1988
task-6 delete task 3!

******IN tick task, the task_index2 = 7
 - ***rtems_clock_get_tod - 05:00:00   12/31/1988
task-7 delete task 4!
^^^^^^IN app task, the task_index2 = 2
 - rtems_clock_get_tod - 05:00:20   12/31/1988
^^^^^^IN app task, the task_index2 = 2
 - rtems_clock_get_tod - 05:00:25   12/31/1988
^^^^^^IN app task, the task_index2 = 2
 - rtems_clock_get_tod - 05:00:30   12/31/1988
```

Fig. 3. User2 delete user1's task without tag engine turned on

```
******IN tick task, the task_index2 = 5
 - ***rtems_clock_get_tod - 05:00:00   12/31/19
CALL instruction tag propagation
tag of addr is = <Task External,Task External,CP=false,WorldReadable=false,Read-Write Entry-point Code Memory>
tag of original pc is = <User 2,User 2,CP=false,WorldReadable=false,Read-Write Data Memory>
new calculated pc tag is = <User 2,Task External,CP=false,WorldReadable=false,Read-Write Data Memory>
new set pc tag is = <User 2,Task External,CP=false,WorldReadable=false,Read-Write Data Memory>

LD_IMM CHECK ERROR when copy bit of source address is set
 own_pc = User 2 does NOT DOMINATE
 own_addr = User 1
88
Unexpected trap (40) at address 0x020019AC
```

Fig. 4. User2 delete user1's task with tag engine turned on

From the information given by the tag engine, the call is successfully made and the new PC's tag is generated correctly ((USER2, TASK EXTERNAL, false | READWRITE | DATA_MEMORY | WORLD_NOT_READABLE)). However the exception is raised on a LD instruction that the Owner field of the PC's tag (USER2) does not dominate the Owner field of the address's tag (USER1). This is because when task 5 tries to delete task 1, it uses the rtems_task_delete directive and passes Task_id[1] to it. Then, rtems_task_delete directive tries to get the specific thread by using Task_id[1], which is tagged with user1's tag, and therefore generates a LD error message.

Although RTEMS is not fully tagged and the tag engine has to be turned on manually in the code, the test case shows that the UI tagging scheme for multiple users is working and can be used to help isolate tasks of different users.

5   Conclusion and Future Work

This paper introduces a design of a new security tagging scheme that enhances access control through least privilege while enabling good system performance. The UI tagging scheme focused on securing RTEMS, a single user, multi-thread model runtime executive. An evaluation of the RTEMS architecture provided a better understanding of what tags can and cannot do. According to the security enhancements that were needed, the tag was designed with three fields: Owner field, Code-space field, and Control-bits field. By using these tags, the system is able to separate RTEMS (i.e., code and data) and user (i.e., code and data), divide RTEMS code into different levels, prevent users from using critical system functions, and protect return values. The combination of Owner field and Code-space field tags represents the security class of the tagged data. With the security classes, lattice, and security rules, the information flow can be controlled in RTEMS.

Modifications of RTEMS source code have also been made to support the tagging scheme. This includes addition of a tag manager which provides tag checking and propagation that can not be done in hardware. Some tagging functions have been inserted into specific RTEMS functions to satisfy special requirements of the tagging scheme, such as setting the copy bit of the ID's tag that is going to be returned from some RTEMS functions. RTEMS has also been expanded from a single user multi-threaded model of execution to a multiuser system. RTEMS now supports the concepts of non-privileged user and superuser, where the superuser has the authority to create, delete, and control non-privileged users. A user manager has been added into RTEMS to support the tagging scheme for multiple users.

5.1   Future Work

This section summarizes the future work that could be conducted as an extension of the security tagging project.

Fully Tag RTEMS Code to Enable RTEMS to Always use Tagging.
Currently, all of the test cases work by enabling and disabling tagging as needed.
Therefore only some of the RTEMS code is tagged. For future work, all of the
RTEMS functions have to be tagged, including libraries. The goal is to have a
tagged RTEMS running from the beginning of system initialization. In addition
to the RTEMS functions, global variables need to be tagged with care. This
is especially true when RTEMS is modified to a multiuser system. Some global
variables can be shared among different users while other global variables cannot,
due to the possibility that they may affect other users or the system. Therefore
these global variables need to be made usable only by a specific user manager.

In addition, the C library functions need to be considered and properly
tagged. Because of time restrictions, not all of the C library functions that are
used by RTEMS can be tagged manually. Therefore software tools will have to
be used to generate a list of the C library functions that are used in the RTEMS
benchmarks. These functions will be given special tags. By doing this, additional
checks will be applied when using these functions, to prevent malicious usage of
the important functions.

The process of tagging the complete RTEMS may be time consuming,
because RTEMS requires a fresh build and installation even with a small change
of the code, which takes around 20 min.

Reduce the Overhead of the Tagging System. Since almost every instruction execution requires tag checking of the source or destination operands' tag,
it increases the overhead of the system. For example, normally, the LD instruction loads values from memory space to registers, but in the UI tagging scheme,
the LD instruction has to check the value's tag and store it as the register's tag
additionally. To minimize the overhead, tags can be cached as many as possible
to speed up the tag checking operations. Another way that could reduce the
overhead of the tagging system is to use a tag compression scheme, and data
and code spatial locality information to reduce the overhead.

Persistent Tags and User-Defined Tagging Rules. The current tagging
model focuses on the protection of code and data from unauthorized access
and modification. It is a first step toward enhanced security tagging, such as
user-defined tags. The support of user-defined tags may require the support
of persistent tags (tags that are maintained between system resets), that may
also be used for multi-processor (or multi-core) execution models and storage of
objects in file systems or other permanent storage.

In addition, the UI tagging scheme only supports fixed tagging rules. In the
future, it would be desirable to have user-defined tagging rules. Another manager
could be implemented to support user-defined tagging rules. However, to be able
to support user-defined tagging rules, the system should provide not only the
interface for users, but protections for the system in case a user tries to do
something that could violate the security of the system.

Port Sample Applications to Evaluate the Performance of the Tagging Scheme. Some sample applications could be ported to RTEMS. These benchmark applications could help evaluate the performance of the UI tagging scheme. This may require additional changes in RTEMS code. For example, the portions of RTEMS and C libraries that are needed by the benchmark applications would need to be tagged. What's more, RTEMS is only compatible with a few applications and none of them are usable for evaluation purposes. Additional efforts are needed to port applications to RTEMS. Based on evaluation results, new methods for improving performance, may be proposed.

References

1. Burroughs Corporation, Detroit 32, Michigan. The Operational Characteristics of the Processors for the Burroughs B5000, revision a, 5000–21005 edn. (1962)
2. Dalton, M., Kannan, H., Kozyrakis, C.: Raksha: a flexible information flow architecture for software security. In: Proceedings of the 34th Annual International Symposium on Computer Architecture, vol. 35, pp. 482–493, May 2007
3. Fenton, J.S.: Memoryless subsystems. Comput. J. **17**(2), 143–147 (1974)
4. Kannan, H., Dalton, M., Kozyrakis, C.: Decoupling dynamic information flow tracking with a dedicated coprocessor. In: Proceedings of the 2009 IEEE/IFIP International Conference on Dependable Systems and Networks, pp. 105–114. IEEE, Estoril, Lisbon, Portugal (2009)
5. On-Line Applications Research Corporation. RTEMS C User's Guide, edition 4.10.1, for rtems 4.10.1 edn., July 2011
6. Qin, F., Wang, C., Li, Z., Kim, H.-S., Zhou, Y., Wu, Y.: LIFT: a low-overhead practical information flow tracking system for detecting security attacks. In: Proceedings of the 39th Annual IEEE/ACM International Symposium on Microarchitecture (MICRO-39 2006), pp. 135–148. IEEE Computer Society (2006)
7. Shioya, R., Kim, D., Horio, K., Goshima, M., Sakai, S.: Low-overhead architecture for security tag. In: Proceedings of the 15th IEEE Pacific Rim International Symposium on Dependable Computing, pp. 135–142. IEEE Computer Society, Shanghai, China (2009)
8. Shriraman, A., Dwarkadas, S.: Sentry: light-weight auxiliary memory access control. In: Proceedings of the 37th International Symposium on Computer Architecture (37th ISCA'10), pp. 407–418. ACM SIGARCH, Saint-Malo, France, June 2010
9. Shrobe, H., DeHon, A., Knight, T.: Trust-management, intrusion tolerance, accountability, and reconstitution architecture (TIARA). Technical report, AFRL Technical Report AFRL-RI-RS-TR-2009-271, December 2009
10. Song, J.: Development and evaluation of a security tagging scheme for a real-time zero operating system kernel. Master thesis, University of Idaho, May 2012
11. Song, J., Alves-Foss, J.: Security tagging for a zero-kernel operating system. In: Proceedings of the 46th Hawaii International Conference on System Sciences (HICSS), pp. 5049–5058, Wailea, HI, USA, January 2013
12. Suh, G.E., Lee, J.W., Zhang, D., Devadas, S.: Secure program execution via dynamic information flow tracking. In: Proceedings of the 11th International Conference on Architectural Support for Programming Languages and Operating Systems, pp. 85–96, Boston, MA, USA, November 2004

13. Witchel, E., Cates, J., Asanovic, K.: Mondrian memory protection. In: Proceedings of the 10th International Conference on Architectural Support for Programming Languages and Operating Systems, pp. 304–316 (2002)
14. Yong, S.H., Horwitz, S.: Protecting C programs from attacks via invalid pointer dereferences. In: Proceedings of the 11th ACM SIGSOFT Symposium on Foundations of Software Engineering 2003 held jointly with 9th European Software Engineering Conference. ACM, pp. 307–316, Helsinki, Finland, September 2003
15. Zeldovich, N., Kannan, H., Dalton, M., Kozyrakis, C.: Hardware enforcement of application security policies using tagged memory. In: Draves, R., van Renesse, R. (eds.) Proceedings of the 8th USENIX Symposium on Operating Systems Design and Implementation, pp. 225–240. USENIX Association, San Diego (2008)

UI Tags: Confidentiality in Office Open XML

Lawrence Kerr[✉]

University of Idaho, Moscow, ID, USA
lawrence.kerr@vandals.uidaho.edu

Abstract. Maintaining confidentiality of data is critical, particularly in need-to-know environments. Dissemination of classified data must be controlled according to user clearance, and rests on the proper tagging of data to ensure appropriate access. The eXtensible Markup Language (XML) provides opportunity for tagging through its extensibility, and as a standard format for data storage, processing, and transmission. Its widespread usage covers a broad range of applications, especially in productivity software such as the Microsoft Office suite. This paper describes the UI Tags Project which presents a strategy for imposing security tags within Office Open XML (OOXML) format documents used with productivity suites. Leveraging the underlying XML of these document types enforces mandatory and attribute-based access control policies. Project development goals include a comprehensive system based on a native XML database which allows users to upload new documents as well as read, edit, or delete existing documents, and controls for derivative classification.

Keywords: Mandatory access control · Attribute based access control · MAC · ABAC · XML · OOXML · Confidentiality · Security tagging

1 Introduction

XML, a markup language for describing a wide variety of data, has become a common means of storing and transmitting information. XML consists of a series of nested elements, each with an associated set of attributes. The elements, attributes, and structure of an XML document is typically defined in a schema that describes each element and attribute, along with data types and legal values for each. Many common document formats are based on XML [1, 2]. The flexibility of XML makes it suitable for many of these applications, as well as many others.

Extending these formats becomes a matter of augmenting underlying XML and schemas. Extension allows insertion of further information. One particular use of this extended information might be the inclusion of security information within a document. This security information is leveraged to determine which users have specific accesses to specific parts of a document, while continuing to allow users to utilize familiar tools for creation and editing of content.

This is the high-level goal of the UI Tags document management project. This project strives to create a means of adding paragraph level tagging to Microsoft Word.docx format documents to enforce mandatory and attribute based access

© Springer International Publishing Switzerland 2016
K. Haltinner et al. (Eds.): CSS 2015, CCIS 589, pp. 19–33, 2016.
DOI: 10.1007/978-3-319-28313-5_2

controls by manipulating the underlying XML directly in an automated fashion. This allows a user to create, edit, and delete document content under security constraints contained within the document itself. UI Tags leverages a native-XML database to facilitate storage and retrieval of tagged documents.

The remainder of this document is organized as follows. Section 2 discusses background research in mandatory access control (MAC), attribute based access control (ABAC), Office Open XML (OOXML), and XML change tracking. Section 3 provides an overview of UI Tags with a number of goals. Sections 4 and 5 describe development stages of UI Tags. Finally, a conclusion with future work is included.

2 Background

One high level goal of UI Tags is to provide a system that supports not only MAC tagging of documents, but also a wider set of ABAC tagging. Tagging builds on Office Open XML standards, with initial targets being the individual paragraphs within tagged documents, while change tracking looks at general approaches for detecting and incorporating changes within a general XML tree.

2.1 Mandatory Access Control

The typical model of an multilevel secure (MLS) environment follows much of the mandatory considerations of the Bell La Padula model [3]. Under this model, system entities are grouped as either objects or subjects. Objects are resources to be accessed. Each object is assigned a security level which conveys its relative sensitivity, represented by the object's security classification. Subjects are users or processes that require access to the objects. Each subject is given a security label as well, referred to here as the clearance level of the subject, or simply level. Both subjects and objects can be additionally associated with some number of compartments. Based on the relationship between the level of an object and the level of a subject, as well as their respective sets of compartments, the policy determines whether to grant or deny a particular access.

The fundamental comparison of levels and compartments is known as the "dominates relationship." Comparison is possible among classifications and clearances as each represents a totally ordered set. A typical set might include a number of possible levels such as:

$$U \sqsubset C \sqsubset S \sqsubset TS$$

Here U (unclassified) is the lowest level. All other levels are higher, or more sensitive, up to TS (top secret) which is the most sensitive. Compartments are not ordered as no individual comparison exists from one compartment to another. Taken together, the level and compartments form a partially ordered set. The dominates relationship uses this partially ordered set to determine if one entity dominates another. To dominate an object, a subject must have a clearance at least as high as the object, while also belong to a superset of the object's compartments. A stronger comparison, strict dominance, requires this same relationship with the additional constraint that the dominating subject has either a higher clearance than the object's classification or at least one additional compartment that the object does not belong to.

Two guiding properties form the basis of access decisions. First, the simple security property states that only subjects which dominate an object are granted read access. Any subjects which do not dominate an object are denied access as this would represent a leak of information to lower levels. In a read only environment this single property suffices, but in dynamic environments where objects are not only read, but created, edited, and removed, a further rule is necessary. The *-property deals with this instance. It states that a subject is only granted write access to dominating objects. This ensures the subject only writes to objects which are at the subject's level or higher. A strong *-property takes this further limiting a user to write only to objects with the same level and compartment set.

One artifact of MAC environments is the potential for polyinstantiation. Polyinstantiation occurs when some object is necessarily described differently at different sensitivity levels [4]. A user may only see one instance, matching his or her level, or a user at a higher level might be able to see one or many lower level representations of the same object. Some have described this as a necessary side effect of maintaining multilevel data, even exploiting it to maintain cover stories for various entities [4], while others have sought to limit or eliminate the presence of polyinstantiation [5].

2.2 Attribute Based Access Control

While a number of different approaches have been proposed in the literature, there does not yet seem to be a clear consensus as to an exact definition or model of ABAC ([6, 7]). A common theme in existing work is the advantage of ABAC in context-aware or pervasive computing, where the identity of a service consumer is not necessarily needed or perhaps even known ([6, 8–11], etc.). ABAC is easily configured and presents the flexibility necessary to handle dynamic environments, though this flexibility comes at increased costs as changing or analyzing permissions can become a complex task as the number of attributes increases [7].

For an attribute-based messaging system, Bobba et al. construct policies from attribute name:value pairs [9]. Access control policies here consist of conditions that when satisfied, grant access to message recipients or recipient groups. A condition is a check on values associated with one or more attributes in disjunctive normal form. These conditions form the policy that in this case governs if a user with a particular set of attributes can send a message based on the attributes of the recipient.

Cirio et al. extend a role based access control (RBAC) model with ABAC [11]. They present the difficulties with a RBAC system such as the static nature of role assignments. ABAC supplements RBAC here, adding flexibility through use of attributes for role determination as opposed to user identity. Attributes are associated with both users and resources, allowing dynamic specification of privileges for resources and association of users with privileges.

Kuhn et al. [7] present a combined role-centric model RBAC-A, where attributes are used to supplement and further constrain an RBAC model. Roles and attributes are distinguished from one another based on whether they are static or dynamic. Attributes that are static, or reasonably static, are used as the basis for roles. These include things such as office location, position, or nationality. They are not likely to change frequently if at all. More dynamic attributes such as time of day are leveraged in the ABAC portion of the combined model. Using static roles and dynamic attributes together can significantly cut down on the number of possible roles and rules. An example system with 4 static attributes and 6 dynamic results in at most 2^4 roles and 2^6 rules, whereas a strictly RBAC or ABAC approach results in as many as 2^{10} roles or rules, respectively.

Jin et al. [6] state the necessity of more clearly and mathematically defining ABAC, while providing a model for ABAC that is capable of expressing other, more traditional models such as mandatory, discretionary, or role based access control. Under this model, each attribute is a function with a specific range that returns a value or set of values for some entity. Entities include users, subjects acting on behalf of users, and objects representing the resources available in the system. Each entity is associated with a finite set of attribute functions which return properties of the associated entity. Policies are constructed using constraints on the values of these attribute functions.

Once the basic entities and attribute sets are defined, four configuration points are defined: (1) authorization policies (2) subject attribute constraints, (3) object attribute creation time constraints, and (4) object attribute modification constraints [6]. Authorization policies return true or false as access is granted or denied. Using this framework, the authors are able to create ABAC policies that adhere to DAC, MAC, and RBAC policies.

2.3 Office Open XML

Office Open XML, or simply Open XML, is a standard that seeks to provide a stable document format while providing all features offered by pre-existing productivity applications [12]. The standard originally appeared as Ecma-376 in 2006, and has subsequently progressed to a fourth edition [13] as well as an International Organization for Standardization (ISO) standard [2]. These standards provide schemas for the markup used in various document types including word processing (WordprocessingML), spreadsheet (SpreadsheetML), and presentation (PresentationML), in addition to a number of features shared between file types including the organization of and relationship between various document components.

Each Open XML file consists of a number of different parts, all collected in a single package. The contents and layout of the package are defined in the Open Packaging Conventions (OPC) section of Ecma-376 [13]. An Open XML file is a package that contains a number of individual XML files referred to as parts that specify document content, markup, features, and relationships between different parts. It relies on ZIP technology to combine the various parts into a single object.

Contents of the package are organized in a hierarchy, with each part having a unique name that includes both the location in the hierarchy and the content name. The name represents a pack URI used for addressing specific parts within the package [2, 13]. Common parts of interest are *document.xml, [Content_Types].xml, app.xml,* and *core.xml.*

For Open XML word processing documents, the *document.xml* part contains the main body of text for the document. The metadata associated with an Open XML document is stored in either *core.xml* or *app.xml,* depending on the nature of the metadata. Open XML standards ([2, 13]) define a metadata schema for the core properties common to all file types in *core.xml,* but *app.xml* is reserved for extended properties - application specific items. The schema for the core properties defines fifteen pieces of information that can be used, including such items as creator, creation date, last modifier, last date modified, subject, title, and keywords. None of the metadata elements is required, and if no data is present, the part as a whole can be omitted. Repetition of elements is not allowed – for example, a document with two creator elements results in an error. Any deviation from what the schema allows in the core properties also results in an error.

The extended properties are application dependent, and allow the incorporation of information beyond the core properties. The same rules apply here – adherence to the schema, non-repeating elements, etc. The schema governing extended properties defines nearly twice as many types as the core properties, including such items as application and version; character, word, paragraph, and page counts; template used; and total editing time.

2.4 XML Change Tracking

In order to support document altering operations, the system must detect changes to both the document content and the underlying XML structure. Changes can then be collected in a delta script, essentially a list of all changes necessary to derive a new version of a document from an original. Traditionally, a "diff" between two files consists of a line-by-line comparison of different files. This works well for many file types, but misses structural information when dealing with XML tree based data [14, 15]. Thus, a number of algorithms deal specifically with the tree structure of XML in detecting and characterizing changes.

Many of these algorithms tend towards the hashing of elements or subtrees of an XML document for the purpose of fast comparisons between documents. In many instances, only leaf nodes of the XML tree are hashed, with interior nodes aggregating the hashes of their descendants, with the hope of providing a means of pruning subtrees from the possible search space.

Khan et al. present an algorithm for change detection that generates signatures for each node in the XML tree [14]. For a leaf node, the signature is computed as a hash of the contents of the node. All other nodes will have a signature that combines the signatures of all the child nodes (in this case using XOR). Comparisons between trees are then only needed if the root nodes differ. Cobena et al. match as large a proportion of the original tree in the edited tree by leveraging unique node IDs [16]. Lindholm proposes a three-way merge algorithm for XML documents [17]. A three-way merge involves an original document, and two replicas of the original that are edited independently. The merge occurs in two stages: (1) each replica is compared to the original, changes are detected, and two deltas are obtained; (2) the deltas are applied to the original, generating a new document that incorporates changes found in each replica. The changes that appear in the delta script are based on changing content of a node, or some structural change (structure here is based on the parent-child relationship in the XML tree). Conflicts are identified as ambiguous conditions where different changes are detected in the same node in both replicas. For example, a node in the original document might contain the text "Hello," where in the replicas it may contain "Hi" and "Bye", respectively. To resolve such conflicts, Lindholm includes the options to either defer resolving conflicts until post-processing, or to allow for some level of "speculative merging" – taking a best guess.

The example provided is a date field in a document's metadata. If two edited replicas of an original have different dates associated with them, which date should be used for the merge? This question is left unanswered.

Rönnau, Pauli, and Borghoff use hashes of individual elements, as opposed to subtrees, to construct a fingerprint [18]. This fingerprint represents the context of an element and consists of the hash of the element and hashes of other elements within a specified radius. The hope here is that an edit operation on a specific element is possible in the presence of other changes – matching some of the fingerprint or context allows determining where an operation takes place. This allows for delta scripts that do not rely on absolute addressing of changes, as well as commutative deltas, where the ordering of operations does not change the end result.

In further work seeking an efficient change detection strategy, Rönnau, Philipp and Borghoff [19] frame the change detection problem in terms of the longest common subsequence (LCS), that is the sequence of leaf nodes of maximum length at a specific depth that appears in both original and edited documents. This algorithm, called DocTreeDiff, consists of three steps. First, hash values of all leaf nodes and their respective depths are computed, from which a LCS is determined. The second step involves inspecting the ancestors of leaf nodes found to be matching. Differences along the path to the root element from the leaf indicate structure preserving changes as opposed to content changes which only occur at the leaves. Finally, the third step investigates nodes for which no match exists in the opposing document – each of these represents an insert or delete operation.

3   UI Tags Overview

The UI Tags project seeks to develop an end-to-end solution which enforces tagging of specific elements within a document, while enforcing MAC and ABAC policies involving read, insert, update, and delete operations on document content. Challenges include management of the document metadata, merging document changes across security levels, and the capacity for queries over a collection of documents to produce new derivative documents.

The UI Tags Project (or simply UI Tags) encompasses a number of objectives, many of which have been addressed in prior studies including work in document-level and hardware-level tagging. Kerr [20] provided early work enforcing tagging in XML documents, using custom schemas to define tags to be used as attributes of various elements. The secure document portion of UI Tags (henceforth referred to as simply UI Tags in this proposal) extends this work to focus on word processing documents based on Office Open XML ([1, 2]), a standard format used by recent editions of Microsoft Word.

The objectives of the secure document portion of UI Tags include:

1. *Enforcement of element level tagging within Office Open XML documents.* The elements tagged depend on the type of Office Open XML document (e.g., word processing, presentation, or spreadsheet) containing the tagged elements. Current focus is on MS Word documents, with paragraph level tagging.

2. *Utilize an XML database for storage and retrieval of tagged documents.* As work moves to utilize OOXML data, a native XML database seems appropriate, as it allows for the individual processing and storage of individual OOXML parts that make up the document.

3. *Richer set of tags.* While mechanisms are in place to support tagging of documents with ABAC tags beyond the necessary MAC tags, these ABAC tags are not yet fully incorporated into the access control decisions.

4. *Tools for original classification.* Original classification is the initial process of classifying information, which is typically limited to specific entities [21]. Having a set of tools that integrates with Microsoft Word (or any other application the original classifier might employ when creating documents) will help greatly with the creation of multilevel documents, specifically limiting the burden of tag creation and application on the user, while ensuring tagging occurs in an appropriate manner.

5. *Derivative classification.* In a Master's thesis at the University of Idaho, Amack [22] extended continuing work on UI Tags adding controls for derivative classification. Derivative classification can occur when information is derived or combined from other sources. Information derived from a classified source needs to bear a like classification, while combining particular low sensitivity items might result in a combination that requires a higher classification.

6. *Read, insert, update and delete operations.* A further objective is the support of a variety of operations on security tagged Office Open XML documents, while adhering to a defined MAC and ABAC security policy. Possible operations include read, insert (a new element), update (the content of an existing element), and delete (removing an element from the document). Read operations are currently supported through eXist-db.

7. *Document change detection and merge.* In support of document-changing operations, the system must be able to merge changes back into the original document, while conforming to the constraints of the security policy.

8. *Document metadata.* One rather interesting observation of Lindholm [17] that required more work was that the document metadata tends to change inconsistently. In our MAC environment, document metadata presents a possible leak of higher-level information to lower levels. The document metadata typically contains information about the document – time created, number of words, creator or last editor – which could be used to infer more sensitive information. This is also critical in the presence of document-changing operations.

9. *Queries and reporting over document content.* The proposed system provides the capacity to dynamically create documents based on user-supplied queries over a collection of documents, while adhering to the security policy and providing provenance for the retrieved data. The documents returned by these queries will essentially be derived documents, and thus subject to derivative classification constraints.

Also desirable here is the ability to specify the provenance information returned from the query.

UI Tags is primarily envisioned as a tool for government environments where an established MAC policy exists, though it could be implemented in any environment where need-to-know determines access. In a government setting, MAC aspects of UI Tags enforce the existing MAC control requirements (users with specific clearances and need-to-know), while ABAC lends a more dynamic access control mechanism (access based on date or time, nationality of user, etc.). Outside government, medical facilities could also benefit from such a system. Here need-to-know relates to care for a patient. Admission or billing staff needs access to patient demographics, but likely does not require the level of detail into a patient's care that a physician requires.

4   UI Tags Phase 1

The initial phase of UI Tags began with mandatory access control for XML documents. Document here are based on a custom XML schema. The schema defines not only the structure of the elements within the document, but also a series of XML attributes representing the security tags. These XML attributes apply to specific XML elements of interest throughout the document. In this case, the user of the system is the subject, and the objects are specific elements within an XML document. Each labeled element bears three attributes. The first two attributes represent the classification and compartments associated with the containing element. To mitigate some editing issues arising in this multilevel environment, a preserve attribute is also used to indicate a need to partially delete an element. This early effort mitigates a number of issues specific to XML while allowing for four basic database operations. The work culminated in a prototype client/server system that allowed a user to perform any of the four basic operations on an XML database while adhering to a MAC security policy.

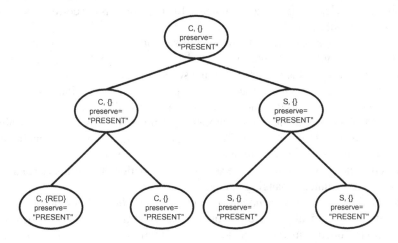

Fig. 1. Example tagged XML tree

Kerr [20] defines four basic operations for security tagged XML documents: (1) read, (2) insert, (3) update, and (4) delete. Each of these operates at the element level within the constraints imposed by both the simple security property and the *- property. For each operation, the path from the root element of the XML tree to the target of the operation is critical – if the path is not fully dominated by the user, there exists the possibility that the element exists as a child of a more sensitive element, essentially orphaning the element in the eyes of the user.

Read access is similar to a Bell La Padula style read, wherein the user must dominate the object. One added attribute, the present attribute, is used here as some editing operations my cause undesirable situations as discussed below. If this flag is present with a value of "REMOVED," any user with a level matching the level of the element flagged as "REMOVED" will not be granted access to the element as it is considered deleted as far as a user of that level is concerned. Consider a user with a confidential clearance, with membership in no compartments. If this user were to request read access to the example XML tree in Fig. 1, only three elements would be allowed: the root element, the left child of the root, and the right child of that child – only those elements bearing at least a C classification with no compartments and a preserve attribute of PRESENT. All data of the higher S classification or any elements with compartment membership are removed from the user's read view.

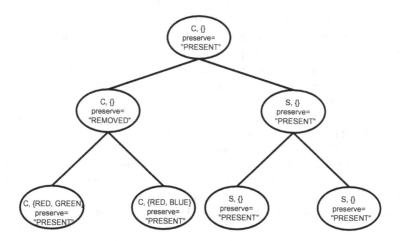

Fig. 2. XML tree with deletion

An insertion operation, where a user adds a new element, has similar concerns. The user's classification must dominate that of the path from the root to the *parent* of where the insertion is to occur. Adopting a strong *-property, the inserted element can only have a sensitivity that matches that of the inserting user's classification. If this requirement is relaxed, two problems arise: (1) a downward flow of information is possible if a high level user inserts a new element at a low level, or (2) a conflict occurs when a low level user attempts to insert an element that may already exist at a higher level. The adoption of a stronger *-property as described above, where insertions are only allowed at the user's classification, prevents this issue. Recalling a C user with no compartments, insertions will only be allowed at any of the three readable elements, provided the insertion bears only the classification and compartments of the inserting user. Any insertion not bearing a C classification with no compartments represents a violation of the strong *-property.

Each of the other types of access involves changing the XML data, either by value of some element or attribute, or its structure as in the cases of adding or removing elements. Deletion of an element presents a number of issues. An element must only be considered for deletion if it is accessible by the user in a read capacity – a user would not realistically need to delete an element that the user is unaware of. So as with a read access, the clearance of the user must dominate the path from the root to the element to be deleted. A confidential user with no compartments would then only be allowed to remove elements tagged with a like classification.

A further consideration involves the content associated with the element. The sensitivity of descendant elements to the deleted element must be considered to ensure only appropriate data is removed. If the clearance of the user performing the deletion dominates the sensitivity of all child trees rooted at the element being deleted, there is no potential for information flow down to lower levels, as any child elements would already be unknown to lower level users. The deletion of an unknown element does not impact a low level user.

If the element contains some child elements strictly dominating the user's clearance, however, the deletion cannot simply remove the element. As the deleting user does not know of the existence of the higher level data, no judgment can be made by the user if the higher level child elements are appropriate for removal. To resolve this situation, a preserve attribute is used to mark the element to be deleted as removed. The setting of this flag must propagate to all descendant elements matching the classification of the deleted element. Once this has been set, the elements "deleted" by the user are no longer visible to a user of that clearance, but remain visible to strictly dominating users. This scenario is shown in Fig. 2, where a confidential user with no compartments has deleted a child element or the root element. As this element has children which the user was not cleared to view (and are thus unknown to the user), the present attribute is updated to REMOVED, effectively removing the element rom the user's view while retaining the more sensitive child elements for higher cleared users.

With an update action, there are two possible scenarios for the update: either a value associated with an element is being updated, or that of an attribute. In the first case, the value of an element is changed (the value here being some child element or some inner data, but not the tag itself). This operation is allowed for subjects with a clearance that is the same as the classification of the element being updated – that is, the subject's level both dominates and is dominated by the level of the object. The path in this case must allow the user to have read access to the element (as an update makes no sense for something the subject cannot read), but does not necessarily determine the ability of the subject to update the accessible element. This allows the value to be changed while avoiding any downward flow of information, and prevents any "blind writes" into higher level data that the subject should not have access to.

The second update scenario, where a subject attempts to update an attribute follows the same logic as an element update, with a few conditions:

1. The classification of the containing element determines the updateability of the attribute.
2. The classification label attribute cannot be changed by a subject as this would represent a potential downward flow of information.
3. Similarly, the compartment attribute cannot be changed.
4. The preserve attribute cannot be added or manipulated directly by users

A further concern here, as with delete, is the possibility of child elements of the edited node that are of a higher classification than the clearance of the user. These children are not visible to the user and therefore subject to loss if we allow the edit to proceed. To overcome this obstacle, we employ a series of steps:

1. Ensure both the simple security property and *-property hold for the node with content being edited.
2. Examine the *MaxDescendant* values for affected child elements. Those with a value that strictly dominates that of the edited element must be retained.
3. Set the preserve attribute to "REMOVED" of those elements with higher max descendants that would be lost by the update.
4. Perform the update to the element, making certain that the "REMOVED" or dominating descendants are retained.

Following these steps, users can edit content of a node in the XML tree without the worry that the edits of a low level might displace any child elements of a higher sensitivity.

5   UI Tags Phase 2

Since the early work of Kerr [20], UI Tags has been extended in a number of ways by coordinated efforts in three different areas: (1) an early cooperative effort among Amack, Bhaskar, and Kerr worked towards a foundational prototype system leveraging a native XML database in which individual word processing documents are stored in compliance with a MAC policy as their individual XML parts; (2) Amack's work on a derivative classification module that operates on documents as they are processed, adjusting tagged paragraphs as necessary based on their content as matched to a set of rules [22]; (3) Bhaskar's extension of the prototype, adding elements of attribute-based access control [23].

UI Tags Phase 2 work began by extending the Phase 1 tagging approach to OOXML based word processing documents. Tagging occurs in the *document.xml* part at the paragraph level, largely as the concept of paragraph exists both in the text content of the document and as a common element in the XML. Most content in the main body of text within the document is contained within paragraph elements. Other more granular elements could be used, though these do not necessarily relate to a logical unit of content in the eyes of the user (text runs, for example, are used to distinguish separate editing events or other application specific artifacts).

In addition to attaching compartments and labels to XML paragraph elements, a set of tags appearing at the beginning of each paragraph's text is also inserted. This allows for persistence of tag information when the document is opened and subsequently saved, as any custom XML markup is removed by MS Word, per a court decision involving a patent on custom XML in Word documents [24].

Using a database for backend storage of XML content led to the selection of native XML database eXist-db [25]. With eXist-db, individual XML parts of an OOXML document can be stored, queried, and retrieved using XPath [26] and XQuery [27] expressions.

On a read request, each individual part of the document is retrieved from the database. Once the *document.xml* part is obtained, a check of each paragraph is conducted, ensuring the requesting user's clearance dominates the classification of the paragraph. If a paragraph is not dominated, it is removed from *document.xml*, resulting in a document containing only those paragraphs a user is allowed to view. In the event there are no paragraphs viewable by the user, no document is returned.

This work provides limited support for edit operations. The prototype is able to determine if change has occurred in a document using a fingerprint scheme similar to Rönnau, Pauli, and Borghoff [18], though this only works on documents that are whole, not in cases where the user is allowed a view of only a subset of the document. In cases where the whole document is available, the edited version simply takes the place of the original – no delta script is generated or applied.

In addition to this issue with change tracking and subsequent merging of different versions, one other concern of interest was identified in the course of this work. First, as mentioned by Lindholm [17], metadata management becomes an issue when merging changes between versions of documents. This is further compounded by the security policy. Document metadata may itself represent a leakage should higher level information be exposed. For example, a document containing paragraphs with a range of classifications is edited by a high level user. If the metadata reflects this change to all users, lower level users are able to view this and may infer the existence of nature of the higher level insertion simply by having the identity of the higher level user.

Building on the UI Tags foundational prototype, Amack [22] developed a means of building and applying derivative classification rules. These rules define specific strings and the classification that paragraphs containing these strings must bear. The need for derivative classification arises when new documents are created based on content in previously classified documents, with the new content requiring classification in a like manner.

Derivative classification is governed by a classification guide that consists of a number of classification rules established by an original classifier [21]. Each rule contains a string that is associated with a specific classification. Should a paragraph contain the indicated string, it is expected that paragraph will be assigned the indicated classification. Amack established an XML format for classification rules in UI Tags [22]. Rule creation is facilitated for the original classifier by a rule builder. As rules are created, they are appended to a rule file stored in eXist-db.

Derivative classification can occur when documents are uploaded to the server as well as when read requests are submitted. In either case, each paragraph is inspected for an occurrence of a classification string in the collection of rules. If a match is discovered, a check for rule expiration is made. Non-expired matching rules result in a check for dominance. Here only rules that result in a new classification that dominates the existing classification are allowed. If the rule indicates a new classification that is non-dominating or non-comparable, the change is marked for review and an error condition explaining the non-dominating result is logged. An original classifier must then review and resolve these issues.

Bhaskar [23] introduced some elements of ABAC to UI Tags. Attributes in this context represent further indicators that supplement the MAC labeling which could include designations such as dissemination and export controls.

Facilitating these ABAC tags presents somewhat of a problem. While the document is being stored and processed, these attributes can be stored in the XML, but for persistence (as they will be removed as custom XML) a new solution is necessary as the addition of further text prepending each paragraph becomes somewhat unwieldy. To resolve this issue, the use of endnotes is used here in conjunction with XML attribute tags. Each paragraph still has the security label prefix on each paragraph, accompanied by a reference to an endnote. In the endnote, where space and readability are not issues, full details on the classification, compartments, and additional attributes are found, allowing for persistence in a way that is familiar to the user. While this provides a means of ABAC tagging, it does not use the tags in access control decisions.

6 Future Work

As UI Tags evolves, a number of areas for further work have emerged. While many of the previously enumerated objectives have been satisfied with prior work, several critical issues still remain. Among these are extending the MAC model to incorporate ABAC features, particularly in how these attributes affect specifically MAC artifacts – the simple security property, the *-property and polyinstantiation. In coordination with extending this model, implementing the read, insert, update and delete operations with support for ABAC constraints is also necessary.

Along with ABAC operation support, metadata management and change tracking are critical. Metadata needs to be managed in such a way as to remain coherent and consistent, but not leak any information to lower levels. While change tracking is supported in a limited way, further work is necessary to adequately track changes under security constraints.

Finally, dynamic document creation work must be completed, whereby a user is able to submit a query, and a document containing relevant results is returned, consisting of information pulled from various documents in the database. These dynamic documents are subject to MAC and ABAC security constraints, as well as derivative classification, and must show sources for all information retrieved.

References

1. Ecma, T.C.: Office Open XML (2006)
2. ISO/IEC 29500-1:2012 - Information technology – Document description and processing languages – Office Open XML File Formats – Part 1: Fundamentals and Markup Language Reference (2012). http://www.iso.org/iso/home/store/catalogue_ics/catalogue_detail_ics.htm?csnumber=61750. Accessed 30 October 2014

3. Bell, D.E., La Padula, L.J.: Secure computer system: Unified exposition and Multics interpretation (1976)
4. Lunt, T.F.: Polyinstantiation: an inevitable part of a multilevel world. In: 1991 Proceedings of Computer Security Foundations Workshop IV, pp. 236–238 (1991)
5. Wiseman, S.: Lies, Damned Lies and Databases (1991)
6. Jin, X., Krishnan, R., Sandhu, R.: A unified attribute-based access control model covering DAC, MAC and RBAC. In: Cuppens-Boulahia, N., Cuppens, F., Garcia-Alfaro, J. (eds.) DBSec 2012. LNCS, vol. 7371, pp. 41–55. Springer, Heidelberg (2012)
7. Kuhn, D.R., Coyne, E.J., Weil, T.R.: Adding attributes to role-based access control. Computer **43**(6), 79–81 (2010)
8. Wang, L., Wijesekera, D., Jajodia, S.: A logic-based framework for attribute based access control. In: Proceedings of the 2004 ACM Workshop on Formal Methods in Security Engineering, pp. 45–55 (2004)
9. Bobba, R., Fatemieh, O., Khan, F., Gunter, C.A., Khurana, H.: Using attribute-based access control to enable attribute-based messaging. In: 2006 22nd Annual Computer Security Applications Conference, ACSAC 2006, pp. 403–413 (2006)
10. Frikken, K., Atallah, M.J., Li, J.: Attribute-based access control with hidden policies and hidden credentials. IEEE Trans. Comput. **55**(10), 1259–1270 (2006)
11. Cirio, L., Cruz, I.F., Tamassia, R.: A role and attribute based access control system using semantic web technologies. In: Meersman, R., Tari, Z. (eds.) OTM-WS 2007, Part II. LNCS, vol. 4806, pp. 1256–1266. Springer, Heidelberg (2007)
12. Ecma Technical Committee 45, "Office Open Xml Overview." Ecma International (2006)
13. Standard ECMA-376 (2012). http://www.ecma-international.org/publications/standards/Ecma-376.htm. Accessed 30 June 2013
14. Khan, L., Wang, L., Rao, Y.: Change detection of XML documents using signatures. In: Proceedings of Workshop on Real World RDF and Semantic Web Applications (2002)
15. Peters, L.: Change detection in XML trees: a survey. In: 3rd Twente Student Conference on IT (2005)
16. Cobena, G., Abiteboul, S., Marian, A.: Detecting changes in XML documents. In: 2002 Proceedings 18th International Conference on Data Engineering, pp. 41–52 (2002)
17. Lindholm, T.: A three-way merge for XML documents. In: Proceedings of the 2004 ACM Symposium on Document Engineering, pp. 1–10 (2004)
18. Rönnau, S., Pauli, C., Borghoff, U.M.: Merging changes in XML documents using reliable context fingerprints. In: Proceedings of the Eighth ACM Symposium on Document Engineering, pp. 52–61 (2008)
19. Rönnau, S., Philipp, G., Borghoff, U.M.: Efficient change control of XML documents. In: Proceedings of the 9th ACM Symposium on Document Engineering, pp. 3–12 (2009)
20. Kerr, L.: Polyinstantiation in multilevel secure XML databases. MS Thesis, Department of Computer Science, University of Idaho, Moscow, Idaho (2012)
21. Executive Order 13526- Classified National Security Information | The White House (2009). http://www.whitehouse.gov/the-press-office/executive-order-classified-national-security-information. Accessed 22 October 2014
22. Amack, A.S.: Automating derivative classification in multi-level secure documents. MS Thesis, Department of Computer Science, University of Idaho, Moscow, Idaho (2014)
23. Bhaskar, D.V.: Software Design Specification for Storing Multilevel Secure XML for Easy Retrieval. University of Idaho, Moscow (2014)
24. Microsoft Corp. v. i4i Ltd. Partnership - Supreme Court (2010). http://www.supremecourt.gov/opinions/10pdf/10-290.pdf. Accessed 25 November 2014

25. eXistdb - The Open Source Native XML Database. http://exist-db.org/exist/apps/homepage/index.html. Accessed 22 October 2014
26. Berglund, A., Boag, S., Chamberlin, D., Fernandez, M.F., Kay, M., Robie, J., Siméon, J.: XML path language (xpath). In: World Wide Web Consort. W3C (2003)
27. XQuery 1.0: An XML Query Language (Second Edition) (2011). http://www.w3.org/TR/xquery/. Accessed 25 November 2014

The Search for Trust Evidence

David E. Ott[✉], Claire Vishik, David Grawrock, and Anand Rajan

Intel Corporation, Chandler, AZ, USA
{david.e.ott,claire.vishik,david.grawrock,anand.rajan}@intel.com

Abstract. Trust Evidence addresses the problem of how devices or systems should mutually assess trustworthiness at the onset and during interaction. Approaches to Trust Evidence can be used to assess risk, for example, facilitating the choice of threat posture as devices interact within the context of a smart city. Trust Evidence may augment authentication schemes by adding information about a device and its operational context. In this paper, we discuss Intel's 3-year collaboration with university researchers on approaches to Trust Evidence. This collaboration included an exploratory phase that looked at several formulations of Trust Evidence in varied contexts. A follow-up phase looked more specifically at Trust Evidence in software runtime environments, and whether techniques could be developed to generate information on correct execution. We describe various research results associated with two key avenues of investigation, programming language extensions for numerical Trust Evidence and an innovative protected module architecture. We close with reflections on industry-university researcher collaborations and several suggestions for enabling success.

1 Introduction: The Problem of Trust Evidence

As the number and diversity of computing devices continues to grow at a rapid pace, there is a need to develop more sophisticated frameworks for establishing trust between interacting devices. Consider, for example, a set of Internet of Things (IoT) devices in the context of a smart city. Devices under the control of a user may wish to connect with peer devices offering information or other services. Likewise, service devices are designed to connect with user devices, either peer-to-peer, directly, or through a gateway. In general, user devices are frequently heterogeneous and the context of interaction is dynamic. For example, mobility may enable a large number of devices to interact in passing as users come and go.

Authentication is one means by which interacting systems may establish a trustworthy relationship. By exchanging private information using a secure communication protocol, a service device may identify a client device (and/or its user) in order to establish trust. Similarly, a client device may use digital certificates or another means to identify the service and establish trust with the service device. Cryptographic or trusted computing methods may be employed to ensure the identification process is robust against man-in-the-middle attacks, spoofing attacks, and other threats to the mutual identification process.

Our reliance on authentication, however, is not without its problems. While authentication approaches may reliably establish the identity of a system and/or its user, they

© Springer International Publishing Switzerland 2016
K. Haltinner et al. (Eds.): CSS 2015, CCIS 589, pp. 34–45, 2016.
DOI: 10.1007/978-3-319-28313-5_3

fail to assess whether the system involved is actually trustworthy. An obvious example is a system infected with malware; while the user may successfully use the system to connect with a service and pass authentication, the underlying device may independently launch an attack against the interacting device, attempt to eavesdrop on private data exchanges, or simply interfere with interaction between the devices. Perhaps less obvious is a device that has been misconfigured, making it vulnerable to malicious attacks or privacy breaches. For example, it may lack appropriate software updates or fail to make use of antivirus software, operating system firewall features, or system security policies. Also of concern are systems that have had failures or compromises that leave them in an unknown state. A system may have sustained a breach by a network bot leaving it in an ambiguous state of health or compromise. Or, a device may have sustained a hardware failure (e.g., hard drive) leaving it in an unknown state that may have security implications or be hard to distinguish from an overt attack.

Besides overlooking the operational state of a device, authentication commonly fails to acknowledge different levels of trust and conditional trust, instead providing a single barrier to entry and all-or-nothing access to promised services and interaction. Instead of allowing provisional interaction until a system's state and operational characteristics can be verified, it ignores all considerations once authentication credentials can successfully be delivered. One might imagine a more sophisticated scheme that requires additional information about the type and state of the system that requests interaction. Similarly, one might image systems that don't require authentication at all for non-private services. However, a system requesting interaction must provide evidence of non-malicious intent and correct operation.

We refer to information beyond basic authentication credentials as Trust Evidence. While the precise definition of Trust Evidence is an open research question, it might include information about:

the authenticity of a device,
a platform's configuration,
patterns of hardware and software operation with respect to normal behavior,
use of security policy or well-recognized security standards and levels,
mechanisms to protect stored secrets,
measures taken to insure message or data integrity, and
past event history, including remediation actions that have been taken.

Trust Evidence may be generated by request from a system wishing to interact, transmitted to the peer system for analysis, and then processed or consumed by the peer system as part of its risk management framework. Two devices may mutually collect Trust Evidence at the onset of an interaction, or periodically as an interaction proceeds and enters different phases of data exchange, each with a different set of security considerations. For example, evidence of secure storage mechanisms may precede the exchange of confidential information. Or, evidence of software updates and versioning may precede software-based service interactions.

Trust Evidence may be used to establish whether a peer device or system is trustworthy, to select a threat posture within an unknown or heterogeneous environment, to dynamically assess the degree of trustworthiness of devices and systems as their software and operational environment changes, and to discover trustworthy devices and systems. Trust Evidence may be seen as a companion to authentication approaches which are still useful in establishing user or system identity, but which need additional mechanisms to assess the actual system participating in the interaction.

Trust Evidence includes many open questions to be investigated by researchers exploring the boundaries of what is possible and desirable in a crowded world of new devices and device types. How might Trust Evidence be defined? How should Trust Evidence be created and transmitted? How might Trust Evidence be consumed? Should Trust Evidence be produced on the fly or stored by a device for future queries? Could Trust Evidence be obtained and stored by a third party who provides profiles as an information service? What is the life span of Trust Evidence? When does Trust Evidence fail to be useful since system and device operation is dynamic and information can become outdated?

2 Exploratory Research

To better understand how Trust Evidence might be formulated and applied to real-world scenarios, Intel sponsored a 1-year university research effort involving several academic teams. Such programs are often referred to by Intel as *seedlings* since preliminary research is needed to better identify the right questions to ask and the most promising approaches for further investigation. In many ways, such programs help to grow the maturity of a research area and better position subsequent researchers for developing usable results.

Research by University of North Carolina [1, 2] looked at techniques for game operators to validate the behavior of game clients in terms of valid execution paths. Their approach makes use of symbolic execution to extract constraints on client-side state as implied by client-to-server messages. Researchers then use constraint solving to determine whether the sequence of client-to-server messages can be verified given possible user inputs, and in light of the server-to-client messages already received. The approach implies that Trust Evidence may be inferred using symbolic execution of known sources code and message histories that either follow or fail to follow expected execution sequences.

Research by UC Berkeley [3] considered the use of a new program representation referred to as a *hybrid information- and control-flow graph* or *HI-CFG*. The representation may be used to study program inputs as they go through complex transformations in order to understand when a system is being manipulated by an attacker and when it is functioning as expected. Researchers leverage this structural understanding to scale program analysis beyond what is feasible with monolithic symbolic execution. The approach uniquely combines both control- and data-flow aspects of a system binary as it executes, and researchers show the efficacy of their approach for applications like a PDF viewer and a word processor. The framework might be used to generate Trust Evidence both within the context of a single system, and by an interacting system that shares a copy of the HI-CFG for a given piece of software.

Research by Dartmouth College [4] looked at how real-world information security practitioners, both developers and security officers, lack the appropriate policy language to provide clear, intelligible, and machine-actionable descriptions of trustworthy behavior. They propose three policy primitives: compositional reasoning, counting primitives, and isolation primitives as SELinux extensions and provide two case study policies to communicate expected process behavior and trust-altering process events. Continued work looks at refining proposed extensions into more formal policy languages and developing quantitative and qualitative metrics to evaluate relative effectiveness in increasing system trustworthiness. The policy language may be used to define and exchange Trust Evidence between interacting systems.

Finally, University of Washington researchers [5] considered interacting devices in the context of a consumer home, including desktops, laptops, wireless routers, televisions, gaming consoles, appliances, healthcare devices, children's toys, and various home automation and infrastructure devices. After cataloging potential attack types and vectors, they present a framework for thinking about device security and risk assessment. The framework includes device security goals (privacy, availability, command authenticity, and execution integrity), digital data goals (privacy, integrity, and availability), and environment goals (environment integrity, activity pattern privacy, sensed data privacy, and sensor validity). Trust Evidence may be defined using their framework, and risk assessment may follow from whether sufficient evidence has been provided to insure each of these aspects.

3   Trust Evidence for Software Runtime Environments

A key outcome of seedling research was the realization that Trust Evidence requires the ability to verify the correct execution of system and application software, and that execution predictability was a central issue.

On the one hand, a framework was needed that could evaluate whether the behavior of a device, directed by system or application software, followed an accepted path or pattern of behavior that is expected. This idea within the program became known as *baselining*. Baselining captures the notion that despite considerable complexity, security-critical execution sequences often follow predictable patterns of control-flow behavior, for example, executing frequent user functions or standard system protocol sequences. This predictability might be captured and used to assess the behavior of a device or system at runtime, and to generate Trust Evidence for system state, operation, and configuration.

The notion of baselining is similar to that of *control-flow integrity* [6] in that it examines the flow of instructions and control at runtime. But while CFI, which makes use of control-flow graphs (CFG), binary analysis, execution profiling, and sometimes static analysis, is interested in strictly enforcing acceptable paths of execution, baselining is a coarser approach that aspires to be more practical. That is, a multiplicity of approaches may be used to define execution reference points, and the goal is to generate evidence of trustworthy execution rather than enforce strictly defined execution paths. In baselining, the degree of conformance to a baseline is an indicator of trustworthiness much like guard rails constrain the direction of travel but not the details of the vehicle's fine-grained movements from lane to lane.

Baselining also borrows from the notion of *anomaly detection* [7], for example intrusion detection systems that build a statistical model of expected network behavior and then use this model to identify suspicious endpoints and communication patterns. Approaches to baselining might similarly develop a model of expected system behavior during software execution, and then apply statistical methods to assess degree of conformance. Trust Evidence may then be cast in statistical terms and describe the degree to which a dynamic system conformed to a control-flow or operational schema defining trustworthy behavior.

The notion of baselining implies the need for a methodology to define reference points for assessing control-flow behavior of a system or device. Another realization by university researchers was the important role that a software developer, administrator, or perhaps even user could play in defining baselines for Trust Evidence. Dubbed *intention semantics* [8], human agents are often in a position to understand and articulate the intended behavior of system and application software as it directs control-flow behavior, and to define what actions are acceptable and within the scope of correct functionality. As such, further research on Trust Evidence should provide avenues for software developers, in particular, to define meaningful baselines that can be used for the generation of Trust Evidence at runtime.

4 Promising Avenues

Intel went on to sponsor a 2-year follow-on initiative enabling university researchers to explore a more focused notion of Trust Evidence that looks at approaches to software control-flow baselining, including methods for defining intention semantics. Here, we describe two of them in some detail: Imperial College London's *pluggable evidence aggregation language* [9–12] and KU Leuven's *protected module architecture* [13–19].

4.1 Pluggable Evidence Aggregation Language

Imperial College London researchers approached the problem of software baselining and intention semantics through a set of programming language extensions to be used directly by software developers to annotate their program code. The extensions allow a software developer to express expectations about the path of execution that their software takes, and to generate numerical Trust Evidence by a runtime system that supports the framework.

Researchers propose three key constructs within their scheme [9]. First is the `expect` statement which defines numerical Trust Evidence values for arbitrary execution paths or portions of program state. An example is as follows:

```
@expect[max] default 0.1 {
    if (calledBy foo1) setTrustEvidenceTo 0.9;
    if (calledBy foo2) setTrustEvidenceTo 0.3;
    if (sameDomain(@caller)) setTrustEvidenceTo 0.8;
}
method foo(...) { ... } // body of method foo(...)
```

In this example, a program variable tracking Trust Evidence is set to a particular value depending on the calling module within the execution sequence. A higher value represents a higher level of trustworthiness during program execution, while lower values express unexpected sequences or sequences that imply greater risk. (Here, 1.0 is seen as maximally trustworthy while 0 is seen as totally untrustworthy.) max is a compositional operator and suggests that the resulting Trust Evidence value should be the higher value between the newly assigned value and a prior existing value.

While expect blocks generate values indicating trustworthy state or control flow behavior, policy blocks are intended to generate actions in response to those values. An example is as follows:

```
@policy{
    grant if (localTrust > threshold)
    deny otherwise
}
```

Here, a policy block compares a local trust variable to a pre-defined threshold in order to decide whether access to a device resource is granted or denied. Blocks like this can be defined with arbitrary, application-specific logic to consider whatever program state, control flow, or execution considerations might be relevant. Researchers often refer to such blocks as *policy decision points* [10].

A third construct is the switch statement [10]. An example is as follows:

```
@switch {
    deny  : (-1,deny);
    incon : (-1,incon);
    _     : ((eval <body>), _);
}
```

The block builds upon the outcome of the prior block. If deny is the decision, then the method should return with the deny message and a payload value of-1. If the decision is inconclusive, then the return message should indicate incon and include a payload value of-1. Otherwise, another program bock is evaluated as indicated. Researchers refer to such blocks as *policy enforcements points* [10] since it is where an evaluated decision is realized. It, essentially, enforces a baseline expectation given the outcome of actual execution.

An interesting feature of the ICL framework is the use of numerical values to represent degrees of control-flow trust and to quantify the trustworthiness of program state and other runtime considerations. The scheme allows for a rich, flexible aggregation framework that can, for instance, test for maximum or minimum values, add values together, computed weighted averages, create statistical profiles across many program iterations, and so on. In fact, programmers are free to invent application-specific Trust Evidence aggregation schemes without constraint. A Trust Evidence profile might be provided to an interacting system by request, or evaluated by the runtime system itself which is designed to protect values against tampering.

Researchers go on to develop a trust calculus language that they refer to as *pluggable evidence aggregation language*, or *Peal$^+$* [12]. The language uses basic conditions (predicates indicating numerical trust or risk scores) and inequalities (statements comparing scores) to create rules, policies, and policy sets. Researchers use the tool PERLT [11] to verify conditions and to determine satisfiability. PERLT operates on statements referring to policies, policy sets, conditions, and domain-specifics. There are two modes of evaluation: verification can proceed explicitly by converting all references to numerical values and then crunching the numbers, or it can proceed symbolically and make use of an SMT solver. Researchers use the well-known Z3 SMT solver in their work, an approach that captures logical dependencies well but constrains the allowable complexity of underlying formulas.

We might imagine the ICL framework to generate Trust Evidence in one of several ways. First, a device may present to a requesting device a single score, or perhaps set of scores, reflecting Trust Evidence evaluations for various layers of a system stack and applications running on that stack. Trusted Computing Group [20] frameworks and standards might be utilized to support hardware isolation of values, secure storage, and attestation support. Alternatively, an interacting device may request an execution profile that includes a history of Trust Evidence values collected over a period of time or in response to a particular input provided by the querying device. The resulting profile may be analyzed by the requesting device, perhaps without disclosing the critical features of interest. A third alternative might be the use of a third party which requests a Trust Evidence profile, analyzes it according to well-understood criteria, and then provides Trust Evidence assessment information on demand.

ICL's work on programming language extensions and numerical trust data provides an innovative approach to Trust Evidence. Its features, in particular, support interesting aggregation and composition functions, and a direct way for software developers to articulate constraints on trustworthy software execution. Future work includes several directions. First, the scheme must be combined with approaches that manage the integrity of Trust Evidence collection and storage within the runtime system, and the communication of Trust Evidence to an interacting system. The protected module architecture described in the subsequent section could serve both of these functions, for example. Second, researchers might develop methodologies and tools for the creation of Trust Evidence values. Many schemes are possible and one might imagine a catalog of approaches that describe how extensions could be applied to various data types, system IO calls, cryptographic processing, and more. Third, research on compilers could address how to translate high-level programming language extensions to binary instruction flows in efficient ways, especially if architecture support for the framework is provided on the underlying system. Finally, researchers may continue to explore practical use cases for demonstrating annotation semantics.

4.2 Protected Module Architecture

KU Leuven researchers propose the use of a protected software module architecture and associated programming paradigms to address baselining, and to realize intention semantics for developers. Trust Evidence follows from attestation features and custom routines designed to provide evidence of correct system operation.

The framework relies on a memory protected software unit that researchers refer to as a *self-protecting module* [13]. Each SPM resides in a protected area of system memory and is comprised of two key components. First is a *public section* where the module's code and non-confidential data can reside. While the contents of this section are potentially readable by other processes on the system, the framework provides integrity guarantees that preclude unauthorized modification, even by system software. Second is a *secret section* which stores the module's private data (e.g., cryptographic keys). Read and write access to the secret section is only possible from within the module itself, a mechanism that provides a high level of assurance.

To insure the integrity of an SPM's public section and the privacy of an SPM's secret section, a special memory access control model is implemented in one of several ways. First, researchers demonstrate that a lightweight hypervisor might be used which divides the system into two virtual machines, a *legacy VM* and a *secure VM*. The former hosts the operating system kernel and user applications while the latter hosts protected modules. A special security kernel also resides in the secure VM that implements fine-grained access control. The architecture, which researchers refer to as Fides [13], implements strictly enforced entry points that prevent operating system and application processes from accessing protected modules against access control policy.

A second approach demonstrated by researchers [15] implements this memory access control architecture as hardware support. Researchers show how extensions to mainstream microprocessors may also be used to effectively isolate protected modules and maintain strict adherence to framework access control policy. In fact, researchers demonstrate that such extensions can be implemented with fairly minimal circuit area requirements, performance overhead, and power demands.

A third approach demonstrated by researchers is that of operating system kernel modifications [14, 18]. Researchers use Linux to show that the memory architecture can be implemented using virtual memory regions that they refer to as *compartments*. Compartments have special access control features implemented using standard MMU features found on most processors. By aligning compartments to memory pages and then configuring read-write properties using standard mechanisms, the system can be configured to generate a page fault when a protected module is accessed. The page fault can then be handled by a kernel extension that implements the protected module architecture control policy.

Researchers point out that their framework maintains its trustworthiness guarantees, even in the face of malware infection on the host system. Attackers are free to use the framework to create malware that runs in protected module space. But, because memory protections mechanisms maintain entry point restrictions, the integrity of additional modules and the confidentiality of their associated secret data is maintained. In fact, their threat model is one that makes very few assumptions about attacker capabilities and doesn't preclude the possibility of malicious code running at user- or kernel-level on the same system.

Compiler support for protected modules is considered in their hardware-based implementation known as Sancus [15]. Researchers show that simple developer hints designating which functions should be protected is enough to apply automated LLVM-based tools that compile standard C files into the protected module architecture automatically.

The compiler will also protect the runtime stack by placing it in the protected module, and it will use an ID scheme to track logical entry points for subsequent reference. Cryptographic techniques are used for secure linking. Modules also clear registers when they exit at runtime in order to avoid information leaks.

An interacting system may build trust in software running on the protected module architecture by making use of cryptographic features built into the framework. The architecture supports secure communication channels and remote attestation that provides a robust method for confirming module identity and integrity. Researchers apply a cryptographic hash to the secure module's public section which can then be reported to an interacting system [14, 18]. Included in the associated security report is also the layout of the module and a cryptographic signature. An instruction for computing the MAC of a protected module is included in the hardware implementation of the scheme [15]. A secure exchange protocol, including a nonce mechanism to counter replay attacks, is used to communicate the value to an interacting system looking to verify the module.

Trust Evidence may also be generated by the use of trust assessment modules running within protected memory regions as protected modules. For example, a trust assessment module may be developed that examines the state of the system's process table, generates a cryptographic hash of system binaries, reports on applications running on the system, summarizes system configuration, or samples an application's call stack as it is running on the system. Modules can be highly customizable and directed at particular aspects of a runtime system. Trusted modules may be designed to interact with another system in specific ways, handling queries and implementing specialized communication and attestation protocols.

KU Leuven's protected module architecture effectively provides a zero-software trusted computing base, or TCB. That is, its protection scheme can be made to work without relying on software running on the device. In fact, it will continue to work even when malicious software is running with kernel level privileges on the system. Its remote attestation features and support for trust assessment modules makes it a strong approach for addressing the problem of Trust Evidence. Future work might include developing an extensive body of programmer tools and methodologies for leveraging protected modules in real-world software and understanding how protected memory implementation approaches map to different device types within IoT and other heterogeneous device contexts.

4.3   Related Work

Execution profiling is described by Elbaum and Munson in [21], although authors focus on the problem of intrusion detection and not Trust Evidence. As mentioned earlier, control flow profiling has been widely explored since then and many of the approaches and results are described in [6]. Some additional approaches to Trust Evidence include mathematical formulations [22, 25], reputation schemes [23], learning models [24], and hybrid frameworks [26].

5 Reflections on Industry-University Research Collaboration

Finally, we close with a few reflections on our industry-university researcher collaborations over the course of the Trust Evidence research program. We believe university research collaboration to be an important avenue for investigating new problem domains and approaches. Through university research, industry sponsors can explore new territory and build the groundwork for future directions in technology. University researchers can be especially valuable in developing new ideas, shedding light on complex problem domains, and proving experimental technologies.

Industry sponsors may find it valuable to employ a variety of program types, and both bottom-up and top-down methods in identifying research areas. Program types might include single investigator projects for highly directed problems, seedling programs for exploring new ideas, and multi-researcher programs for investigating complex challenges and challenges that require interdisciplinary approaches. Bottom-up approaches to identifying research areas give technical teams across the industry organization an opportunity to communicate technology gaps that could benefit from university research collaboration. Top-down approaches give company leaders an opportunity to identify new directions that can benefit from initial investigation by university researchers.

Industry sponsors may find it useful to structure their collaboration with university researchers in various ways. Annual workshops or retreat events help to summarize program results for a broad audience and to foster discussion between researchers. Industry visits to university labs can lead to a deeper understanding of research challenges and strengthen relationships with university graduate students who are at the heart of the research effort. Monthly seminars with rotating speakers can be valuable, especially if industry participants can also contribute perspectives. Finally, regular research meetings (e.g., weekly or biweekly) can be valuable for close-knit collaborations and during periods of pivotal decision-making.

References

1. Bethea, D., Cochran, R.A., Reiter, M.K.: Server-side verification of client be-havior in online games. ACM Trans. Inf. Syst. Secur. **14**(4), 32 (2011)
2. Bauer, L., Liang, Y., Reiter, M.K., Spensky, C.: Discovering access-control misconfigurations: new approaches and evaluation methodologies. In: Proceedings of the 2nd ACM Conference on Data and Application Security and Privacy, February 2012
3. Caselden, D., Bazhanyuk, A., Payer, M., McCamant, S., Song, D.: HI-CFG: construction by binary analysis and application to attack polymorphism. In: Crampton, J., Jajodia, S., Mayes, K. (eds.) ESORICS 2013. LNCS, vol. 8134, pp. 164–181. Springer, Heidelberg (2013)
4. Bratus, S., Locasto, M., Otto, B., Shapiro, R., Smith, S.W., Weaver, G.: Beyond SELinux: the Case for behavior-based policy and trust languages. computer science Technical report TR2011–701, Dartmouth College, August 2011
5. Denning, T., Kohno, T., Levy, H.: Computer security and the modern home. Commun. ACM **56**(1), 94–103 (2013)
6. Abadi, M., Budiu, M., Erlingsson, U., Ligatti, J.: Control-flow integrity principles, implementations, and applications. ACM Trans. Inf. Syst. Secur. **13**(1), 4 (2009)

7. Chandola, V., Banerjee, A., Kumar, V.: Anomaly detection: a survey. ACM Comput. Surv. **41**(3), 15 (2009)
8. Vishik, C., Ott, D., Grawrock, D.: Intention semantics and trust evidence. In: Information Security Solution Europe (ISSE), November 2012
9. Huth, M., Kuo, J.H.-P., Sasse, A., Kirlappos, I.: Towards usable generation and enforcement of trust evidence from programmers' intent. In: Marinos, L., Askoxylakis, I. (eds.) HAS 2013. LNCS, vol. 8030, pp. 246–255. Springer, Heidelberg (2013)
10. Huth, M., Kuo, J.H.-P.: Towards verifiable trust management for software execution. In: Huth, M., Asokan, N., Čapkun, S., Flechais, I., Coles-Kemp, L. (eds.) TRUST 2013. LNCS, vol. 7904, pp. 275–276. Springer, Heidelberg (2013)
11. Huth, M., Kuo, J.H.-P.: PEALT: an automated reasoning tool for numerical aggregation of trust evidence. In: Ábrahám, E., Havelund, K. (eds.) TACAS 2014 (ETAPS). LNCS, vol. 8413, pp. 109–123. Springer, Heidelberg (2014)
12. Huth, M., Kuo, J.H.-P.: On designing usable policy languages for declarative trust aggregation. In: Tryfonas, T., Askoxylakis, I. (eds.) HAS 2014. LNCS, vol. 8533, pp. 45–56. Springer, Heidelberg (2014)
13. Strackx, R., Piessens, F.: Fides: selectively hardening software application components against kernel-level or process-level malware. In: ACM Conference on Computer and Communications Security(CCS), October 2012
14. Avonds, N., Strackx, R., Agten, P., Piessens, F.: Salus: non-hierarchical memory access rights to enforce the principle of least privilege. In: Zia, T., Zomaya, A., Varadharajan, V., Mao, M. (eds.) SecureComm 2013. LNICST, vol. 127, pp. 252–269. Springer, Heidelberg (2013)
15. Noorman, J., Agten, P., Daniels, W., Strackx, R., Van Herrewege, A., Huygens, C., Preneel, B., Verbauwhede, I., Piessens, F.: Sancus: low-cost trustworthy extensible networked devices with a zero-software trusted computing base. In: 22nd USENIX Security Symposium, pp. 479–494, August 2013
16. De Clercq, R., Schellekens, D., Piessens, F., Verbauwhede, I.: Secure interrupts on low-end microcontrollers. In: 25th IEEE International Conference on Application-specific Systems, Architectures and Processors (ASAP 2014), June 2014
17. Agten, P., Jacobs, B., Piessens, F.: Sound modular verification of C code executing in an unverified context. In: Proceedings of the 42nd ACM SIGPLAN-SIGACT Symposium on Principles of Programming Languages (POPL 2015), January 2015
18. Strackx, R., Agten, P., Avonds, N., Piessens, F.: Salus: kernel support for secure process compartments. EAI Endorsed Trans. Secur. Saf. **15**(3), 30 (2015)
19. Patrignani, M., Agten, P., Strackx, R., Jacobs, B., Clarke, D., Piessens, F.: Secure compilation to protected module architectures. ACM Trans. Program. Lang. Syst. **37**(2), 6:1–6:50 (2015)
20. Trusted Computing Group. http://www.trustedcomputinggroup.org
21. Elbaum, S., Munson, J.C.: Intrusion detection through dynamic software measurement. In: Proceedings of USENIX Workshop on Intrusion Detection and Network Monitoring, April 1999
22. Wang, Y., Singh, M.P.: Evidence-based trust: a mathematical model geared for multiagent systems. ACM Trans. Auton. Adapt. Syst., September 2010
23. Huynh, T.D., Jennings, N.R., Shadbolt, N.R.: An integrated trust and reputation model for open multi-agent systems. J. Auton. Agents MultiAgent Syst. **13**(2), 119–154 (2006)
24. Fullam, K., Barber, K.S.: Dynamically learning sources of trust information: experience vs. reputation. In: Proceedings of the 6th International Conference on Autonomous Agents and MultiAgent Systems (AAMAS) (2007)

25. Wang, Y., Hang, C.-W., Singh, M.P.: A probabilistic approach for maintaining trust based on evidence. J. Artif. Intell. Res. **40**(1), 221–267 (2011)
26. Yu, H., Shen, Z., Leung, C., Miao, C., Lesser, V.: A survey of multi-agent trust management systems. IEEE Access **1**, 35–50 (2013)

Cloud and Device Security and Privacy

Surrender Your Devices or Be Turned Away: Privacy Rights at the Border

Elizabeth J. Etherington[✉]

University of Baltimore, Baltimore, MD, USA
Elizabeth.J.Etherington@gmail.com

Abstract. Recent revelations of mass surveillance programs used by the National Security Agency has triggered a shift in concerns over the information that we carry in our portable electronic devices remaining private. The public is becoming more protective of their personal information and apprehensive regarding who collects, stores and uses it. One major area of concern is that of information being carried with international travelers becoming subjected to a search without a search and seizure warrant at our nation's ports of entry. Under the Border Search Doctrine, found within our Fourth Amendment, agents have the right to search inbound travelers for contraband, which is generally considered reasonable for the state to do to protect its citizens. However, when this doctrine is applied to electronic devices, the amount of information that likely would be accessed is vast and variable, potentially triggering our Fourth Amendment protection. This article discusses the standards of privacy under the Fourth Amendment, its border search doctrine, issues surrounding self-incrimination, other challenges, and a possible legislative solution that could protect passengers' information as it passes through a port of entry into the United States.

Keywords: Surveillance · National security agency · Homeland security · Border patrol · Privacy · Fourth amendment · Fifth amendment · Self-incrimination · Electronic device · Cloud computing

1 Introduction

Our society is becoming ever more mobile, with the average American carrying a cellular phone, smart phone, tablet or laptop with them at any given moment. When traveling internationally, Americans often carry more than one mobile digital devices with them either for personal or business reasons. Within these devices are held vast amounts of data of varying types the scope of which is often unbeknownst to the user. Since the revelations of the National Security Agency's mass surveillance programs by Edward Snowden in 2012 [1], the public's concerns regarding the privacy of their electronic personal information have heightened, triggering public resistance and a re-examination of instances of potential privacy violations by the Supreme Court. International travelers crossing into our country briefly lose their right to privacy at the border, requiring that, if chosen, their persons and property be searched for contraband by Border Patrol Agents, Transportation Security Agency, both of which the Department of Homeland

© Springer International Publishing Switzerland 2016
K. Haltinner et al. (Eds.): CSS 2015, CCIS 589, pp. 49–56, 2016.
DOI: 10.1007/978-3-319-28313-5_4

Security. Should a traveler refuse to comply, they could be denied entry into the United States.

The emergence of cloud computing has brought to light many questions regarding jurisdiction, ownership, and content protection at the border. There is a need for the Supreme Court to re-examine and rule on the privacy issues that border searches present, particularly with portable electronic devices that are so commonly part of a traveler's belongings.

2   Brief History of the Fourth Amendment and the Border Search Doctrine

One of the fundamental grievances the American colonists held against the English Crown was the lack of privacy protections for English Citizens. The Crown had the right to issue a writ of assistance, which gave an agent the right to kick in the door of a citizen's home, then search and seize anything that could incriminate the owner without much limitation [2]. This concern was addressed in our Constitution's Bill of Rights as the Fourth Amendment, giving American citizens protections against unreasonable searches and seizures by the government, without a warrant specifically outlining the state's reasonable suspicion and probable cause for the invasion of privacy. These protections "draw a firm line at the entrance to the house" and extend to a citizen's person, papers and effects [3]. Today, the average American's effects include portable electronic devices containing enough information to fill a warehouse [14].

Given the legal requirement for a search warrant, there are some exceptions to this strict rule. The Fourth Amendment allows agents of the law to search and seize evidence under specific conditions, such as when there are certain exigent circumstances, the evidence can be seen in plain view, agents are in hot pursuit of their suspect, and during administrative and border searches.

Border searches raise particular concern because, once a border patrol agent has admittance into the device, their access is potentially limitless. However, the Court has reasoned that this doctrine is reasonable because the government has an interest in preventing unwanted persons and effects access its borders. The Court specifically reasons that border searches are the country's best defense against the introduction of contraband, thus border agents have been granted complete authority to conduct routine searches and seizures at the border [9]. Essentially, searches made at the border are pursuant to the time-honored tradition of the sovereign's right and responsibility to protect itself and its citizens by examining all persons and effects that are entering into its borders. Such searches can occur without any suspicion [3], and are reasonable simply by virtue of the fact that they are happening at the border [8].

Since 9/11, the Department of Homeland Security has been leveraging this exception to focus on portable electronic devices for evidence of terrorist activity, reporting that it is a very popular way that terrorists, potential terrorists and sympathizers carry their evidence in and out of the country [11]. Along with evidence of terrorism, DHS is also searching for other contraband, including human rights violations, weapons smuggling, espionage, immigration violations and child pornography. Child pornography, in particular, is mainly transported and shared in a digital format and often found while searching devices traveling into the US from Mexico [7].

Regardless of these findings, privacy advocates often argue that because of a portable electronic device's great capacity to store information, a random or suspicion-less search would have a greater impact on the owner's privacy than when searching, for example, luggage [15]. Luggage can only contain so many effects, but accessing a person's electronic device can give the border agent theoretically unlimited access to a person's private information and innermost thoughts at any given moment. Once an agent has access to a person's device, there is no current regulation regarding the type of information that can be viewed during the search, including privileged attorney-client information, HIPAA, Privacy Act of 1974 data, etc., thus many judges have begun to advocate for restrictions on the government's authority to view any content on any device crossing the border [7].

3   Cloud Computing and Border Searches

The latest trend in the computing industry is "cloud computing", which is the use of third-party servers to store and access data and system infrastructure anywhere in the world. Cloud computing has become a popular tool for large-scale companies as well as individuals, because it is easy to procure, easily accessed, inexpensive, and can instantly be stretched to meet most demands [4]. The average public consumer may not know the actual location of the physical servers, and it is possible for the data to be stored in multiple locations at any given moment. For example, users of Gmail, Google's free email service, have access to their emails from any location, but the emails may be stored in a location known only to Google [7].

Cloud computing raises a plethora of privacy concerns for individuals entering the U.S. border because the technology is so young that the courts have not had time to develop an argument and firmly define its Fourth Amendment protections. The border search doctrine allows an agent to search persons and properties physically present at the border. One could argue that data stored on the hard drive of a portable electronic device that is crossing the border is considered "physically present", thus can be searched freely, and without suspicion. Can the same be said for material that is stored in the cloud which can be accessed by the device that is present at the border? Since the information can be accessed from any device, using any internet connection in the world, does the government have to wait for a physical device to cross the border, or can one argue that the data is already inside the border? Does an individual even know where their data is physically stored?

4   Court's Historical Approach

Until recently, the Courts have been interpreting the Fourth Amendment in a manner that draws on the historical application of the law. For example, one can look to Smith v Maryland [10] for guidance. In 1978, Maryland State Police were trying to establish that Smith was calling the telephone inside a home that he was suspected of robbing.

To confirm their theory, they requested that the telephone company, without a search warrant place a pen-register, or a type of wiretap that captures the telephone numbers that are dialed out from the line, on his home telephone line. On appeal, Smith argued that his privacy had been infringed upon, but the Supreme Court ruled that there is no privacy in telephone numbers, reasoning that the users of the telephone must know that they are disclosing the information about who they are calling to the phone company, a third-party service provider, when they voluntarily make the phone call.

Cloud computing can be analogous to Smith v Maryland because the information that an individual stores on the third party server has been voluntarily surrendered to the third party. Essentially, the government could argue that if one wants their data kept private, they should keep it to themselves, rather than hand it over to someone else for storage.

However, the Fourth Amendment also distinguishes between content and non-content data, also known as "metadata". Metadata is data about data, such as telephone numbers and the length of the telephone call. Police officers in Smith v Maryland were correct in their assumption that a search warrant was not needed to gather telephone numbers coming from the defendant's home, because metadata is not considered private. Thus, under this ruling, the border patrol officers are allowed to know that the person crossing the border has data stored in the cloud, which services are being used, and how much data is being stored.

Conversely, the Fourth Amendment protects content, or the substance of the phone calls that were made by the defendant in Smith v Maryland. The first Supreme Court case to put privacy restraints on content data was the landmark case US v Katz [6], where, in 1966, Katz, who was working as a bookie, stepped into a telephone booth to make a phone call, closed the door behind him, and placed coins into the machine before dialing the telephone number. Unbeknownst to him, police had mounted a "listening device" to the outside of the booth and recorded his end of the conversation. On appeal, the Supreme Court took up the issue of protecting the content of a transmission over a telephone wire, laying out a two part test: (a) the individual exhibits a subjective expectation of privacy, and (2) that expectation of privacy is one that society is prepared to distinguish as "reasonable". The Court reasoned that Katz's actions of stepping into a booth and closing the door behind him was an expectation of privacy that society would recognize as reasonable, as it was not very likely that a random person from the public would try to push in through the door to listen. Rather, a person would wait their turn to use the telephone, giving Katz his space and privacy to finish his call.

5   Court's Contemporary Approach

The conclusions of the courts have varied greatly on the legality of suspicion-less searches of portable electronic devices crossing the border, fluctuating between comparing the searches to that of a closed, and sometimes locked, container, to being akin to the physical search of a person. For example, in United States v Arnold, Customs and Border Protection (CBP) agents seized Arnold's computer after selecting him for secondary questioning and viewed child pornography while manually searching the machine for several hours. Upon appeal, Arnold claimed that the search had infringed upon his privacy and dignity. However, the court decided that the search of a piece of property could never implicate the dignity that a search of the physical person would. The court specifically described the laptop as analogous to a physical container, effectively stating that the "balance of interests in a border search of property would always favor the government" [9].

Another example of a warrantless search at U.S. border checkpoint is the recent U.S. v Cotterman case. In the spring of 2007, Cotterman and his wife traveled from Mexico to the port of entry in Lukeville, Arizona, where a check of his passport revealed to CBP officers that he had a criminal record involving minors and sexual conduct. A second alert instructed the officers to be on the "lookout" for the possibility of child pornography to be in his possession. Because of the alert, Cotterman's vehicle was searched revealing two laptops, one belonging to his wife, and one to him. Cotterman offered his password to give the officers access, but his help was refused out of fear that he would delete evidence. Instead, the laptop was forensically examined in a crime lab over a period of a few days. Analysis found over three hundred of child pornography hidden in the unallocated space, but Cotterman fled to Sydney before he could be arrested.

Finally, in 2009, when Cotterman was apprehended and charged in connection with the images discovered on his laptop, he argued that the search was particularly offensive due to the amount of time the forensic analysis took, the copies of his hard drive that were made, the lack of reasonable suspicion, and the fact that his machine was removed from the checkpoint and taken to a secure location. The court held that reasonable suspicion was not necessary because the search satisfied the Fourth Amendment's border search exemption, and that the forensic examination was done with "reasonable diligence and speed" [8].

However, in the Opinion, the Court asked "what are the limits upon this power of technology to shrink the realm of guaranteed privacy?" It expressed the need for a reasonableness requirement because of technology's dual and conflicting capabilities to decrease privacy, while simultaneously increase the expectation of privacy that society is currently struggling with [14]. This is not trivial, because it is the first mention of applying reasonable suspicion to the border search exception.

6   Self-incrimination, Encryption and Passwords

Americans are protected against self-incrimination by the Fifth Amendment, which states that "[n]o person... shall be compelled... to be a witness against himself". Within the borders of the country and under certain circumstances, a person cannot be forced to testify against themselves and, for example, surrender a password to unlock a device. However, until very recently, this protection was not afforded to travelers passing through the nation's port of entries.

In 2006, Sebastian Boucher was searched at the border and compelled by court order to surrender his password to render an encrypted drive on his laptop searchable after evidence of child pornography was found [5]. Boucher argued for his Fourth and Fifth Amendment privacies, but the Court ruled that he could be compelled, because authorities did not want the password for the content of the password, but rather to search the device. He did not have to give the actual password, he just had to unlock the device, effectively separating the contents of the password from the contents of the device.

Once compelled, Boucher argued that by decrypting the drive he would be testifying that he, as opposed to some other person, had place the contents on the hard drive, encrypted the contents, and could retrieve and observe said contents at his leisure. The court did not agree, saying that the act of decryption is not testimony.

However, in 2012, the Supreme Court reversed its opinion, citing three components to the Fifth Amendment; compulsion, an act of testimonial communication, and incrimination, all of which can be found in Boucher's case. They said that, "even if the decryption and production of the contents on the hard drives themselves are not incriminatory, they are a 'link in the chain of evidence' that is designed to lead to incriminating evidence: this is sufficient to invoke the Fifth Amendment" [5]. Essentially, the production of evidence explicitly or implicitly conveys some statement of fact.

Circuit courts have yet to directly address the role of encryption and password protection, but it seems reasonable that such protections would have little effect on preventing border agents from obtaining information from a portable electronic device. According to the U.S. District Court for the Western District of Texas, "A password on a computer does not automatically convert a routine search into a non-routine search. A password is simply a digital lock". The court goes on to reason that it is common for travelers to place locks on their luggage, yet they are "subject to 'routine' searches all the time" [7]. In the case of Cotterman, the court failed to address the legality of federal agents circumventing the appellant's password.

7 Challenges at the Border

There is a unique set of challenges a passenger may face while traveling into the United States with internet integrated portable electronic devices. Often, the user's data is held on remote servers, rather than the device itself. There are instances where neither the traveler nor the Border Patrol Agent will know if the data they are looking at is stored on the device itself, or a remote server. If it is in the cloud, how can we tell if the data is actually at the border? Could it be in a foreign country? Do our laws pertain to access? We must ask who else's privacy will be infringed upon who has access to the data, but is not presently at the border.

When overturning Cotterman's ruling in 2012, the Supreme Court found that a digital device is a "conduit to retrieving information from the Cloud, akin to the key of a safety deposit box", and that the "virtual safety deposit box" may not itself cross the border, it may appear as a unified part of the device when obtained at the border [14]. Fundamentally, the traveler's cache is just a click away from the eyes of an agent of the State.

The Court also found that when a traveler is packing their luggage and papers, they can easily pick and choose what items to take with them, and which to leave at home. When traveling with a mobile device, removing files unnecessary to their future trip is and "impractical solution given the volume and often intermingled nature of the files." It is time consuming and potentially ineffective [14].

A third major issue that the Supreme Court discussed in its 2012 opinion is the potential for data mining without the traveler's knowledge. According to a Privacy Impact Assessment for the Border Searches of Electronic Devices done by the DHS, travelers are not required to be told that information found on their devices has been copied for a later analysis [16]. The Court poignantly stated that, "International travelers certainly expect that their property will be searched at the border. What they do not expect is that, absent some particularized suspicion, agents will mine every last piece of data on their devices or deprive them of their personal property for days... or longer".

8   Legislative Resolutions

In light of the revelations regarding NSA's mass surveillance, the public's concern over privacy and government eavesdropping is more intense than it has been in generations. The fact that overwhelming amounts of personal information is bared to the prying eyes of the government would, and should, be a cause for concern among American citizens [13].

The proposed Securing Our Borders Act of 2011 could offer guidance on what future legislation could look like. The Bill was introduced to the House of Representatives in December of 2012, but neither the House nor the Senate has taken any action on it [12]. It would set forth rules requiring that any searches of electronic devices at the border done by the State be based on reasonable suspicion, in addition to the border search exception. Guidance on the additional constitutional justification was vague, but the imposition of probably cause would be the next step in obtaining a search warrant, and would provide substantial protection for individual privacy.

9   Conclusion

Given the public's increasing concern over privacy rights and the government's exposure of mass surveillance programs, in addition to the rising number of mobile devices crossing into our nation's borders due to their popularity and economical access, the Supreme Court must consider the privacy implications surrounding electronic storage and cloud computing. While one can argue that limitations must be placed on our border patrol agents' scope and authority to search, it can also be argued that the nation has the right to protect its citizen by keeping out unwanted materials. While the capability to view the contents of portable electronic devices crossing into our borders exists, we must ask ourselves if the capability should be limited. Simply because we can do something may not mean that *should* do it. The Courts must find a balanced approach to our nation's safety and privacy.

Acknowledgments. Special appreciations to Pablo Breuer for the constant sounding board and leading to trust my own mind; Joshua Rosenblatt for sending me feedback until the night before presentation; Ebrima Ceesay for his advice and convincing me to pursue publication; Zachariah Abraham for his swift red-ink edits, Barry Grant for all his support, and Patrick Preller and David Mabry for inspiring my interest in our privacy laws.

References

1. Breslow, J.M.: How edward snowden leaked "thousands" of NSA documents, 13 May 2014. Public Broadcasting Service: http://www.pbs.org/wgbh/pages/frontline/government-elections-politics/united-states-of-secrets/how-edward-snowden-leaked-thousands-of-nsa-documents/
2. Chicago, T.U.: The Founder's Constitution, Amenment IV, Document 2, vol. 5. Univeristy of Chicago, Chicago (2000). http://press-pubs.uchicago.edu/founders/documents/amendIVs2.html
3. Corbett, P.E.: The future if the fourth amendmend in a digital evidence context: where would the supreme court draw the electronic line at the international border? Miss. Law J. **18**(5), 1263–1308 (2012)
4. Hurwitz, J., Bloor, R., Kaufman, M.: Cloud Computing for Dummies: HP Special Edition. Wiley Publishing Company, Indianapolis, Indiana (2010)
5. In re Grand Jury Subpoena to Sebastian Boucher, No. 2:03-mj-91, 2009 WL 424718 (United States District Court for the District of Vermont, 19 Feburary 2009)
6. Katz v. United States, 389 U.S. 347 (Supreme Court of the United States 1967)
7. Lotrionte, N.: The sky's the limit: the border search doctrine and cloud computing. Brooklyn Law Rev. **78**, 663–695 (2013)
8. McKnight, A.: Privacy rights left behind at the border: the exhaustive, exploratory searches effectuated in unites states v. cotterman. Brigh. Young Univ. Law Rev., 591–606 (2012)
9. Nadkarni, S.: Let's have a look, shall we? a model for evaluating suspicionless border searches of portable electronic devices. UCLA Law Rev. **16**, 148–194 (2013)
10. Smith v. Maryland, 442 U.S. 735 (Supreme Court of the United States 1979)
11. Sternstein, A.: Judge says border officials can search you laptop and cellphone, 31 December 2013. Nextgov: http://www.nextgov.com/defense/2013/12/judge-says-border-officials-can-search-your-laptop-and-cellphone/76130/
12. Summary H.R. 6651–112th Congress, Washington D.C, 12 December 2011–2012
13. Townsend, S.A.: Laptop Searches at the Border and Unites States v Cotterman. Boston Univ. Law Rev. **94**, 1745–1779 (2014)
14. US v. Cotterman, 709 F.3d 952 (9th Circuit 2013)
15. Vijayan, J.: Justices let stand appeals court decision on border searches of laptops, 14 January 2014. Computer World: http://www.computerworld.com/s/article/9245368/Justices_let_stand_appeals_court_decision_on_border_searches_of_laptops
16. Winkowski, T.S., Kibble, K.C., Callahan, M.E.: Privacy impact assessment for the border searches of electronic devices. U.S. Department of Homeland Security (2009)

Comparing Encrypted Strings

Jim Buffenbarger[(✉)]

Boise State University, 1910 University Drive, Boise, ID 83725, USA
`buff@cs.boisestate.edu`

Abstract. Database outsourcing, also known as database as a service, has become a popular way to store and process large amounts of data. Unfortunately, remote data storage can compromise confidentiality. An obvious solution is to encrypt data, prior to storage, but encrypted data is more difficult to query. We describe and demonstrate an efficient scheme for comparing ciphertexts, corresponding to arbitrary plaintexts, in such a way that the result is the same as if the plaintexts had been compared. This allows queries to be processed remotely and securely. Comparison is not limited to equality. For example, encrypted employee names can be sorted remotely without decryption. Any encryption algorithm can be used. Demonstration queries are shown in SQL.

Keywords: Databases · Security · Encryption · Queries · Comparison

1 Introduction

Physically remote databases, whether hosted on a single powerful server, or in a cloud environment, enjoy significant performance benefits [6,10]. They also pose security challenges. The remote site may be untrusted (malicious) or untrustworthy (careless) [2,7,8]. A widely accepted solution is for a client to encrypt and decrypt at least some of the data. The remote site cannot decrypt the encrypted data. However, to fully utilize the computing resources of the remote site, encrypted data must be relationally comparable [1,4,9]. For example, employee names in a database may need to be selected and sorted, before query results are returned to the client, even though the names are encrypted.

We will be making some assumptions, which are not universally held:

- We are only concerned with maintaining data confidentiality, like [1]. We do not want other users, or administrators, of the remote database to be able to determine the plaintext of the encrypted strings stored in the database. We ignore the possibility that they might augment, alter, or delete stored data or query results. We also ignore encrypting metadata and/or schema.
- We want to allow a user to employ any encryption scheme they wish (e.g., AES or DES), like [8] and unlike [1]. A related requirement, recognized in [1], is that adding a new encrypted string to the database should be easy and should not require reencryption of other strings.

© Springer International Publishing Switzerland 2016
K. Haltinner et al. (Eds.): CSS 2015, CCIS 589, pp. 57–66, 2016.
DOI: 10.1007/978-3-319-28313-5_5

- We ignore attacks on the chosen encryption algorithm, including statistical and traffic-analysis attacks.
- We want to allow encryption at only the finest level of granularity. Rather than encrypting entire tables, columns, or rows, we want to allow a user to encrypt the content of each cell in a column independently, like [6] and unlike [5].
- We assume that the order in which a user encounters previously unprocessed strings, which need to be encrypted and added to the database, is reasonably random. This assumption ensures good performance, but has no effect on correctness or confidentiality. If this does not happen naturally it can be arranged. For example, a user who wants to store a previously sorted sequence of strings in a database should shuffle them first.
- We assume that the only operations required for encrypted strings are the common binary relational operators (e.g., "less than"). This allows selection of ranges and sorting. It does not allow general pattern matching (e.g., with the SQL LIKE operator).
- We want comparison to be accurate, with no false negatives or false positives.

The rest of the paper is organized as follows. Section 2 formalizes the problem to be solved, Sect. 3 describes previous attempts to solve the problem, Sect. 4 presents our solution, Sects. 5 and 6 give examples, Sect. 7 considers performance, Sect. 8 describes a cloud-based application of our solution, and Sect. 9 concludes the paper.

2   Problem

We want to store encrypted character strings in an untrusted database, and use queries that compare the strings, without allowing queries to decrypt the strings. Comparison for equality is trivial; relational comparison is more difficult.

Suppose we have two character strings s and t, and a normal (e.g., lexicographic) less-than function:

$$lt : String \times String \rightarrow Boolean$$

(This notation means that the function name is ¡, it takes two string-valued arguments, and returns true or false.) Also, suppose we have encryption and decryption functions:

$$enc : String \rightarrow String$$

$$dec : String \rightarrow String$$

Our goal is to define a function:

$$lt_e : String \times String \rightarrow Boolean$$

that does not use dec such that:

$$lt_e(enc(s), enc(t)) = lt(s, t) \tag{1}$$

In other words, lt_e compares two encrypted strings, returning true if and only if the plaintext of the first is less-than the second, without decrypting them.

3   Related Work

The literature describes two general approaches to solving this problem: order-preserving encryption [1–5] and bucketing [6–8]. Both have limitations.

Order-preserving encryption schemes employ specialized (i.e., nonstandard) encryption algorithms. They allow two ciphertexts to be compared directly, giving the same result as comparing the corresponding plaintexts. Such schemes usually only work with numeric data, but a subset (i.e., prefix-preserving schemes) work with any data. They are immune to false negatives and false positives. Unfortunately, prefix-preserving schemes have been shown to be insecure. Some order-preserving schemes require, *a priori*, all plaintexts as inputs.

Since we are assuming that a user wants to employ a standard encryption scheme (e.g., AES or DES), order-preserving encryption (OPE) schemes are not acceptable.

Bucketing schemes partition plaintexts into sets (i.e., buckets) and assign an identifier (i.e., a tag) to each set. Buckets and tags are chosen such that comparing two tags approximates comparing plaintexts from their respective buckets. Ciphertexts and tags are maintained as a crypto-index, allowing approximate comparison without decryption. Unfortunately, tag-assignment methods have been shown to make these schemes insecure. Furthermore, bucket sizes greater than one cause false positives. Not surprisingly, bucketing can be transformed to prefix-preserving encryption.

Since we require confidentiality, and immunity from false negatives and false positives, bucketing schemes are not acceptable.

4   Solution

We begin by defining two computing domains (e.g., hosts). Let T be the *trusted* domain, with access to *enc* and *dec*. Let U be the *untrusted* domain, without access to *enc* and *dec*. T is the client that wants to store encrypted strings in a database maintained by U.

Let S be the set of plaintext strings used by T.

Trusted T maintains a map, named *ord*, from encrypted strings to comparable values:

$$ord : String \rightarrow String$$

with keys (i.e., domain):

$$K = \{\, enc(s) \mid s \in S \,\}$$

and data (i.e., range) such that:

$$(\forall s, t \in K \mid lt(dec(s), dec(t)) = lt(ord(s), ord(t)))$$

We'll call elements of the range *ordinals*.

Untrusted U keeps an up-to-date copy of *ord*, perhaps as a table in its database. Of course, *ord* $\neq$ *dec*, for security. Indeed, T will need to construct *ord* independently of *enc* and *dec*. We'll see how, below.

Now, when U needs to compare two encrypted strings s and t, from its database, it uses:

$$lt_e(s, t) \equiv lt(ord(s), ord(t))$$

This is the implementation of requirement (1).

To help maintain ord, T secretly maintains an ordered map (e.g., a C++ `map` or a Java `TreeMap`):

$$sec : String \rightarrow String$$

U does not have access to sec. The keys of sec are S, the set of plaintext strings used by T. Its data is such that:

$$(\forall s \in S \mid sec(s) = ord(enc(s)))$$

Now, when T encounters a new plaintext string s, which it needs to encrypt for transmission to U, it performs the following steps:

1. From sec and s, it computes r and t, such that r is the previous key and t is the next key, according to lt. This is easy, since sec is ordered.
2. From $sec(r)$ and $sec(t)$, it computes a, such that:

$$lt(sec(r), a) \wedge lt(a, sec(t)) \tag{2}$$

   In other words, a is an ordinal between the ordinals for r and t, according to lt. A simple algorithm for computing a is described below.
3. It adds (s, a) to sec.
4. It adds $(enc(s), a)$ to ord, and transmits the addition to U, so U can update its copy of ord.

Ordinals, the data values of sec, can be computed as character strings of binary digits. Such a string can represent a real number between zero and one (exclusive), by prefixing the string with a radix point. Thus, for any two adjacent keys r and t in sec, we have two binary numbers, with this real-arithmetic relationship:

$$0.sec(r) < 0.sec(t)$$

We can compute a, their average, from the strings, in time linear to their length, such that:

$$0.a = \frac{0.sec(r) + 0.sec(t)}{2}$$

guaranteeing requirement (2).

Referring to step 1, above, if there is no previous and/or next key, the binary values zero and/or one (respectively) are used.

An ordinal is not computed from its corresponding plaintext or ciphertext. Indeed, two completely different sets of plaintexts could produce the same set of ordinals. Ordinals are computed from the order in which plaintexts are initially encountered, perhaps as a database is initially loaded. This order can be assumed or made reasonably random. Thus, an ordinal preserves its plaintext's confidentiality.

Nevertheless, providing a potential attacker with *any* ordering information about ciphertexts reduces security in certain threat models [14]. From that paper:

- "The primary appeal of OPE is the fact that it offers the ability to encrypt data in a way that allows searches to be performed without possession of the secret key."
- "However, OPE offers truly practical efficiency, and is in fact one of the very few available scalable crypto-computing tools."
- "As discussed earlier in this paper, it is impossible, or, at best, extremely difficult, to design a complex usable system which relies on OPE and achieves provable security."
- "We have also shown that this vulnerability is inherent with the use of OPE."

5   Example: Ordinals

To demonstrate the computation of ordinals, we can construct *ord* and *sec* for a randomized sequence of Dickens titles:

sec	
s	*sec*(*s*)
a christmas carol	001
barnaby rudge	01
david copperfield	01001
great expectations	0101
martin chuzzlewit	011
oliver twist	1
the olde curiosity shop	101
the pickwick papers	11

ord	
enc(*s*)	*ord*(*enc*(*s*))
Ex9jjt3fFGrrwmJ...	01
PWw1d4kFkbTHvb2...	11
SuCLwmRSfX.8dZu...	01001
TtCyN2qxWUUDVlr...	101
ZIq2lKnVaycIo25...	011
cX1Qb3uH2cNWETt...	001
cgvURFXGd2ZjJak...	0101
kGQghEqYKyPzqDr...	1

For example, the hypothetical encryption of:

david copperfield

is:

SuCLwmRSfX.8dZu...

Encrypted strings in the left column of *ord* can be compared by comparing ordinals in the right column of *ord*. Note that the *sec* entries have been sorted for presentation purposes only.

6   Example: Queries

Continuing the example, a remote SQL database might have these two tables, named `titles` and `ords` (respectively):

```
+--------------------+
| title              |
+--------------------+
| Ex9jjt3fFGrrwmJ... |
| PWw1d4kFkbTHvb2... |
| SuCLwmRSfX.8dZu... |
| TtCyN2qxWUUDVlr... |
| ZIq21KnVaycIo25... |
| cX1Qb3uH2cNWETt... |
| cgvURFXGd2ZjJak... |
| kGQghEqYKyPzqDr... |
+--------------------+
```

```
+--------------------+-------+
| enc                | ord   |
+--------------------+-------+
| Ex9jjt3fFGrrwmJ... | 01    |
| PWw1d4kFkbTHvb2... | 11    |
| SuCLwmRSfX.8dZu... | 01001 |
| TtCyN2qxWUUDVlr... | 101   |
| ZIq21KnVaycIo25... | 011   |
| cX1Qb3uH2cNWETt... | 001   |
| cgvURFXGd2ZjJak... | 0101  |
| kGQghEqYKyPzqDr... | 1     |
+--------------------+-------+
```

Suppose the client would like to construct an encrypted query on the encrypted database corresponding to this unencrypted query:

```
SELECT * FROM titles
  WHERE title BETWEEN
   'david copperfield'
     AND
   'oliver twist'
  ORDER BY title;
```

This is the encrypted query:

```
SELECT @lo:=ord FROM ords
  WHERE enc='SuCLwmRSfX.8dZu...';
SELECT @hi:=ord FROM ords
  WHERE enc='kGQghEqYKyPzqDr...';
SELECT T.* FROM titles T, ords O
  WHERE T.title=O.enc AND O.ord
    BETWEEN @lo AND @hi
  ORDER BY O.ord;
```

It produces:

```
+--------------------+
| title              |
+--------------------+
| SuCLwmRSfX.8dZu... |
| cgvURFXGd2ZjJak... |
| ZIq21KnVaycIo25... |
| kGQghEqYKyPzqDr... |
+--------------------+
```

which would be decrypted by the client into the equivalent of:

```
+--------------------+
| title              |
+--------------------+
| david copperfield  |
| great expectations |
| martin chuzzlewit  |
| oliver twist       |
+--------------------+
```

Notice that a client's queries do not require the client to access *ord* or *sec*. Indeed, a client that only needs to read from the database, not update it, need not store *ord* or *sec* at all. There might be many read-only clients, and only one read-write client. A read-only client can therefore be lightweight, in the sense that it need not store the large *ord* and *sec* tables. It need only encrypt queries and decrypt results. This is also why cleint queries are constructed from encrypted strings, rather than ordinals.

An alternative to maintaining a separate table for ordinals, in the remote database, is to prefix each string (e.g., encrypted title) with its ordinal and a separator character. Such aggregates could be compared directly.

7   Overhead

This scheme is not without time and space overhead. The client must check *sec* to determine when a new string is encountered, updating *ord* and *sec*, and

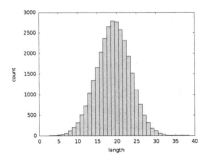

Fig. 1. Ordinal lengths for randomized city/state names

notifying the server, when it happens. Furthermore, to process a query, the server must consult *ord*. Constructing a query, on the client side, requires encryption, but neither *ord* nor *sec* need be consulted.

Assuming commonly available data structures, adding a new string to *sec* requires $O(\log n)$ time on the client, where n is the number of encrypted strings, and an INSERT operation on the server. Consulting *ord* on the server is a JOIN operation.

Collectively, *ord* and *sec* require the client to store one copy of each plaintext or encrypted string, and one copy of its ordinal. This could be a significant amount of data, but only one or a few of a table's columns might be encrypted. We are exploiting, primarily, the server's query performance, rather than its storage capacity.

If strings are encountered in order, according to *lt*, pathological behavior results, as with an unbalanced binary search tree. Ordinals would very long.

If strings are encountered in random order, as we might expect or arrange, much better behavior results. For example, when processing the 30,116 uppercase city/state names in a U.S. zip-code list [13], in random order, the distribution of ordinal lengths shown in Fig. 1 was observed.

The average ordinal length was about twenty. Notice that an ordinal can be shorter than its corresponding plaintext or ciphertext. If desired, byte-to-bit packing could also be employed to compress each ordinal to an eighth of its original length.

Server-side space requirements are not really relevant.

8   In the Cloud

In order to get a concrete feeling for the performance overhead of our solution, we created a MySQL database using the RDS service from Amazon Web Services [11].

First, we created a 3.8 million line dataset, from two publicly available datasets [12,13], containing a line for every street, city, state, and zip code in the United States. From this plaintext file, we created a partially encrypted version, where just the street was encrypted, along with a 1.1 million line file containing the corresponding ciphertext/ordinal pairs. These three files were then imported into the database as tables. The (encrypted) street was the ciphertext/ordinal table's primary key.

We then submitted two queries, analogous to the two title-oriented queries above, with profiling enabled. We asked for the streets with names starting with our state's name: those between "IDAHO AVE" and "IDAHO WAY" (encrypted, when appropriate). The query then sorted the output by street name and zip code. There were 400 such streets. The plaintext query usually took about 10 s. The encrypted query usually took about 50 s.

9 Conclusion

Powerful remote database services have become a popular way to store and process large amounts of information. When the remote environment is insecure, confidentiality can be ensured by encrypting data prior to transmission and storage. To fully benefit from remote computing resources, encrypted data must be relationally comparable in the remote environment. We have shown a secure, accurate, simple, and efficient scheme for doing this. Any encryption algorithm can be used. The *ord* map is essentially an index, as in the bucketing schemes, but unlike those schemes, *ord* is a one-to-one relation to provide accuracy, and tags are assigned to preserve confidentiality.

References

1. Agrawal, R., Kiernan, J., Srikant, R., Xu, Y.: Order preserving encryption for numeric data. In: Proceedings of the 2004 ACM SIGMOD International Conference on Management of Data (2004)
2. Amanatidis, G., Boldyreva, A., O'Neill, A.: Provably-secure schemes for basic query support in outsourced databases. In: Barker, S., Ahn, G.-J. (eds.) Data and Applications Security 2007. LNCS, vol. 4602, pp. 14–30. Springer, Heidelberg (2007)
3. Boldyreva, A., Chenette, N., Lee, Y., O'Neill, A.: Order-preserving symmetric encryption. In: Proceedings of the 28th Annual International Conference on Advances in Cryptology: The Theory and Applications of Cryptographic Techniques (2009)
4. Chung, S.S., Ozsoyoglu, G.: Anti-tamper databases: processing aggregate queries over encrypted databases. In: Proceedings of the 22nd International Conference on Data Engineering Workshops (2006)
5. Elovici, Y., Waisenberg, R., Shmueli, E., Gudes, E.: A structure preserving database encryption scheme. In: Jonker, W., Petković, M. (eds.) SDM 2004. LNCS, vol. 3178, pp. 28–40. Springer, Heidelberg (2004)
6. Hacigumus, H., Iyer, B., Li, C., Mehrotra, S.: Executing SQL over encrypted data in the database-service-provider model. In: Proceedings of the 2002 ACM SIGMOD International Conference on Management of Data (2002)
7. Hore, B., Mehrotra, S., Tsudik, G.: A privacy-preserving index for range queries. In: Proceedings of the Thirtieth International Conference on Very Large Data Bases, vol. 30 (2004)

8. Li, J., Omiecinski, E.R.: Efficiency and security trade-off in supporting range queries on encrypted databases. In: Jajodia, S., Wijesekera, D. (eds.) Data and Applications Security 2005. LNCS, vol. 3654, pp. 69–83. Springer, Heidelberg (2005)
9. Song, D.X., Wagner, D. Perrig, A.: Practical techniques for searches on encrypted data. In: Proceedings of the 2000 IEEE Symposium on Security and Privacy (2000)
10. Swaminathan, A., Mao, Y., Su, G.-M., Gou, H., Varna, A.L., He, S., Wu, M., Oard, D.W.: Confidentiality-preserving rank-ordered search. In: Proceedings of the 2007 ACM Workshop on Storage Security and Survivability (2007)
11. AWS: Amazon Relational Database Service, http://aws.amazon.com/rds
12. AWS: Twilio/Wigle.net Street Vector Data Set. http://aws.amazon.com/datasets/Geographic/2408
13. AggData: Complete List of United States Zip Codes. http://www.aggdata.com/node/86
14. Koleshnikov, V., Shikfa, A.: On the limits of privacy provided by order-preserving encryption. Bell Labs Tech. J. **17**(3), 135–146 (2012). wileyonlinelibrary.com

Social Implications of Networked
and Mobile Applications

Can I Live? College Student Perceptions of Risks, Security, and Privacy in Online Spaces

Kristin Haltinner[✉], Dilshani Sarathchandra, and Nicole Lichtenberg

University of Idaho, Moscow, ID, USA
khaltinner@uidaho.edu

Abstract. This study explores U.S. college students' perceptions of risk, security, and privacy in online spaces, and the strategies used by students to manage online risks. Twenty-one students participated in in-depth interviews and shared their experiences with online spaces and their perceptions of cyber threats. Our findings indicate that student cybersecurity concerns are shaped mainly by routinization and ritualization of risk, optimistic bias, and self-efficacy. Strategies commonly employed to overcome risks include accessing sources that are perceived as credible and trustworthy, restricting information sharing, and exercising learned helplessness—or, what we term here as the "can-I-live syndrome."

1 Background

Due to increased applications of science and technology in society, social science research has shifted its focus towards potential risks associated with scientific and technological developments. Scholars such as Beck (1992) and Giddens (1999) have categorized the contemporary [Western] society as a "risk society." In a "risk society," individuals and groups are often organized in response to unknown and/or unintended consequences of novel risks (e.g., genetic engineering, nanotechnology). As such, a risk society is inherently linked to modernization and the accompanying risk-benefit calculations that drive individual and group behavior. In such a society, individuals are concerned not just with risks for themselves, but for the environment and for future generations.

Online spaces provide ample fodder for creation of novel risks that individuals in contemporary societies are required to deal with, in their day-to-day lives. At a minimum, this is true for the Western industrialized world where computers and the Internet have become a necessity of everyday life. Evidence suggests that these technologies and associated risks are becoming increasingly relevant to peripheral countries as well. As people spend more time in online spaces, they are more likely to be vulnerable to cyber threats. Additionally, time spent in online spaces and familiarity with technology is likely to alter public perception of risks associated with the cyberspace (Campbell et al. 2007).

Having recognized these nuances, computer scientists and researchers have long conducted investigations on physical and cyber-based control systems that are relevant to risk assessment and risk management (e.g., Jones and Ashenden 2005; Ralson, Graham and Hieb 2007). On the other hand, social scientific investigations have focused

K. Haltinner et al. (Eds.): CSS 2015, CCIS 589, pp. 69–81, 2016.
DOI: 10.1007/978-3-319-28313-5_6

broadly on public perception of risks. Research concentrations include identification of social meanings attached to risks, as well as how citizens understand, approach and respond to online risks, security, and privacy concerns. As computer scientists and social scientists have focused on distinct aspects of cybersecurity concerns, a notable gap has developed between the goals of those engaged in the computer industry and the understandings and concerns of the day-to-day Internet users. This presents a great opportunity for interdisciplinary collaboration on areas related to cybersecurity.

Having recognized this gap in the extant literature, in this study we examine user perceptions of online risks and explore how those perceptions differ from formal risk assessments. The study focuses exclusively on U.S. college students, who are part of the millennial generation: the first generation to have experienced cyber technology throughout their life span (Madden and Rainie 2015). In the next section, we briefly review the relevant social science research on cybersecurity, followed by a discussion of our study participants, research methods, and analytical techniques. We then discuss our results and conclude with some suggestions for potential ways to develop "conscientious cybercitizens."

2   Overview of Social Science Research on Cybersecurity

A significant portion of recent empirical investigations has focused on college students' perceptions and behaviors, which is the focus of this paper. College students provide a good population for this line of research, as they tend to use the Internet more than the average American (U.S. Chamber of Commerce Foundation 2012). Furthermore, today's college students/millennials (born between 1980 and 1999) are the first generation for which the Internet has always been a way of life (Madden and Rainie 2015). Prior research on college student perceptions and behavior in online spaces has primarily focused on four areas—Internet overuse and addiction, cyber bullying, effects of Social Network Sites (SNSs), and cybersecurity awareness.

2.1   Internet Overuse and Addiction

College students are particularly vulnerable to overuse of the Internet, which sometimes leads to Internet addiction, i.e. "pathological use" (Kandell 1998). Researchers argue that several factors including psychological and development characteristics of late adolescence/young adulthood, easy access to the Internet, and increased social expectations for regular computer use can lead to potentially problematic cases of overuse and addiction. Overuse can also result due to ready access to SNSs, which college students and young adults (aged 18 to 29) tend to populate more often than other age groups in the U.S. (Pew Research Center 2014). Some scholars have reported that individuals experience feelings of anxiety, depression, or emptiness when they are cutoff from SNSs (e.g., O'Keeffe and Clarke-Pearson 2011; Moreno et al. 2014). Morahan-Martin and Schumacher (2003) posits that, among undergraduate students, those who self-identify as 'more lonely' tend to be drawn online more often and use the Internet as a way to modulate the negative emotions associated with loneliness.

2.2   Cyber Bullying

Due to the increasing prevalence of technological devices such as smart phones and their potential for misuse, some empirical studies have focused on cyber bullying among college students. In one study, Dilmac (2009) asserts gender differences in self-reports of cyber bullying and victimization rates. In this study males reported more cyber bullying behavior than females. Aggression (engaging in behavior such as attacking or hurting others) and succorance (soliciting sympathy, affection, and emotional support from others) were positively associated with cyber bullying, whereas intraception (attempt to understand one's own behavior or the behavior of others) was negatively associated with cyber bullying. Other studies too have reported various effects of cyber bullying on college students such as depression, anxiety, paranoia, suicidal thoughts and/or attempts (e.g., MacDonald and Roberts-Pittman 2010; Schenk and Fremouw 2012).

2.3   Effects of Social Network Sites

In the realm of Social Network Sites, many studies have focused on the aforementioned relationship between SNSs and cyber bullying, anxiety, depression, etc. Additionally, some have focused on the impact of SNSs on social capital as it pertains to college student populations. In one study Ellison, Steinfeld and Lampe (2007) demonstrated a strong association between use of Facebook (a popular Social Network Site) and three types of social capital—bridging social capital, maintained social capital, and bonding social capital. Ellison et al. (2007: p. 1143) argue that Facebook use positively impacts psychological wellbeing, giving "greater benefits for users experiencing low self-esteem and low life satisfaction." In another similar study, Valenzuela, Park, and Kee (2009) found positive relationships between intensity of Facebook use and college students' life satisfaction, social trust, civic engagement, and political participation. However, the researchers qualified the findings by stating that effect sizes for civic engagement and political participations were small and could not be considered as a panacea for youth engagement in civic duty and democracy.

As far as privacy concerns on SNSs are concerned, overall research findings suggest that college students are more risk seeking and/or complacent than risk-aversive. Students are more likely to have private profiles if their friends and roommates do so (e.g., Debatin et al. 2009). Women are more likely to have private profiles than men (e.g., Lewis, Kaufman, and Christakis 2008; Debatin et al. 2009; Lawyer and Molluzzo 2011). Users continually negotiate and manage the tensions between perceived privacy risks and expected benefits (Ibrahim 2008; Debatin et al. 2009). Ibrahim (2008: p. 251) characterize online networks as "complicit risk communities where personal information becomes social capital which is traded and exchanged." Since the creation and preservation of social capital depends on voluntary disclosure of private information to a virtually unlimited audience, SNS users tend to engage in risk seeking behavior and take liberties with disclosing private information, more often than individuals who are not members of online social networks (Fogel and Nehmad 2009).

2.4 Cybersecurity Awareness

Lastly, some studies on college student behavior have focused on issues of awareness, in particular, how lack of awareness about cybersecurity affects safe online practices. This line of research posits that, students are mostly unaware of online dangers (e.g., Lawyer and Molluzzo 2011); students do not receive sufficient education about Internet safety in college (e.g., Lawyer and Molluzzo 2011); and students think that online dangers are more likely to happen to their peers than to themselves (e.g., Campbell et al. 2007). In general, even when people report being aware of online dangers, they are less likely to take precautions in their daily online practices (e.g., Livingstone 2008; Tufekci 2008).

In results presented below we add to this rich extant social scientific literature on college student perceptions of online risks by (1) identifying ways in which students characterize risks, and (2) shedding light on strategies employed to overcome risks. Overall, we argue that three aspects of the risk experience predominantly shape student perceptions of cybersecurity; routinization and ritualization of risk, optimistic bias, and self-efficacy. Additionally, we find that students navigate risky online environments using three main strategies; accessing sources that they perceive as credible and trust-worthy, restricting information sharing, and exercising learned helplessness (i.e., can-I-live syndrome). We provide some potential solutions and suggest areas for future scholarly investigation.

3 Methodology

Data for this study were collected over the 2014-2015 academic year and included 21 in-depth interviews with college students at a large public university in the Pacific Northwest. The interviews ranged from 20 to 60 min in length.

To recruit participants, the research team produced a list of active classroom-based undergraduate courses at the university, excluding classes with fewer than 15 students. Using a random number generator, we systemically selected courses from this list. We then emailed faculty members and asked to come to a class meeting to describe our project and ask for volunteer participants. 40 % of the faculty members agreed to allow us to visit their classroom. In total, we recruited students from 31 classrooms in 22 different disciplines. Courses included 100 level courses (n = 14), 200-level courses (n = 2), 300-level courses (n = 7), and 400-level courses (n = 8). Students were offered extra credit in one course, English 258, which resulted in a high number of participants (n = 6) from this course. Our overall sample consisted of twelve females and nine males. Additionally, the sample consisted of four first-year, three second-year, four third-year, five fourth-year and two fifth-year students. Three of the students did not indicate their standing.

Interviews were semi-structured: they followed an interview guide but were conversational in style. The interviewer began by asking participants about their comfort with, and knowledge of, technology and cybersecurity. We then proceeded to ask participants about their experience with different types of cyber-attacks and their personal actions to prevent cybersecurity violations. The interview guide can be found in Appendix A.

After reading through the data multiple times, searching for emergent themes, we developed a codebook and an analytic frame using standard inductive analysis (Silverman 1985). Once the coding framework was fully developed, we coded all the data for patterns and negative cases.

Limitations of our methodology include allowing participants to self-select into the study. Self-selection could lead to people with stronger views dominating the sample. A second concern is the size of our sample, as we only interviewed 23 students. However, it was clear from the project that we had reached saturation in data collection at the conclusion of 23 interviews. Other methodological concerns include recall bias (errors caused by differences in accuracy and/or completeness of the information recalled by the participants), and social desirability bias (tendency of interview and survey participants to answer questions in a manner that will be perceived favorably by the researchers).

4   Results and Discussion

4.1   Student Characterizations of Risk/Risk Perception

Our data highlighted three frameworks that students used to explain and/or justify the risky actions they took online. We classified these justifications as: routinization and ritualization, optimistic bias, and self-efficacy. When using routinization and ritualization, participants generally allude to their familiarity with the risks and rationalize their behavior by explaining that other people they know act in similar ways. Furthermore, they argue that other people have not fallen victim to online crimes. For example, one student explains why she feels comfortable downloading Internet apps and materials from crowd-sharing sites, in the following way:

> I always think things like Spotify… you just know a lot of people have it and so there's not really like a perceived risk of it being "oh, I shouldn't do that." So, kind of just like those popular ones. I don't wanna say I do what everyone else does, but I do the ones that are more popular, it doesn't seem like there is a lot of risk behind it.

Generally, students rationalize their risky behavior by comparing themselves to their peers who have taken similar actions, and have remained safe. People's behavior is strongly influenced by what sociologists call their reference group: a group of people to which they compare themselves. Reference groups can take three forms: "groups which serve as comparison points, groups to which men aspire, and groups whose perspectives are assumed by the actor" (Shibutani 1955). Thus, not only is it the case that people seek to be similar to or better than those to which they compare themselves, but they are often driven to adhere to a value and behavior system that they imagine people like them share. This theory has shown powerful influence in one's decision making. For example, Ariely (2009) finds that people are far more likely to cheat (or perform unethically) if others in their in-group (those with whom they identify and compare themselves to) also perform and are successful with those behaviors. In contrast, if they see people who are not considered as part of their reference group (i.e., out-group) perform those same actions, they are less likely to follow suit.

A second justification is an adaptation of what social psychologists often refer to as 'optimistic bias' (i.e., the perception and belief that positive events are more likely to happen and negative events are less likely to happen to one's own self). In this context, students are aware that other people have had problems with cybersecurity, but deny that they can similarly be victimized. Indeed, student claims include:

I have a Mac and I've just never had a virus, and I haven't been worried about it.

I think it is probably a risk, but I'm not worried. I've never saw hackers going after me, like old people who don't know what they are doing online, or like rich people who didn't notice that a million dollars got lost.

People simply assume that they are somehow different than those who have been victimized. One clear example of this bias is seen in the case of smoking: Arnett (2000) found that though most participants know that smoking is addictive and can lead to death, most do not believe that they will be harmed by consuming cigarettes for a long period of time. They also believe that they can easily quit. Counterintuitively, optimistic bias has been shown to increase as one gains additional knowledge on a subject (Al-Najjar et al. 1998; Frewer et al. 1998; Chapin and Coleman 2009; Luo and Isaacowitz 2007; Walker et al. 2007). This may be related to how optimistic bias increases with one's perception that they have control over a situation (Helweg-Larsen and Shepard 2001). As college students have grown up with computers, it is likely that they feel they have an elevated degree of knowledge about computer use and thus can control the dangers online.

Optimistic bias is deeply linked to the third justification for risky online behavior, which is couched in ideas of student self-efficacy. Students believe that it is obvious or "stupid" errors that lead to people being victimized. As a result, they trust that they have the level of knowledge and intelligence necessary to protect them.

I feel pretty safe online, just because I can tell the difference between a prince from Egypt, or whatever, who wants my money, and a company that has stuff I want to buy.

If it looks like it was made by a 90 s computer, I don't trust it. If it looks like it was made by a company I can sue, should any actual problems arise, that's how I feel safer.

These examples reflect a related tendency that many people have: to believe that they are better or more skilled than others in managing decisions that involve uncertain outcomes—a practice termed as "self-serving," "self-enhancing," or "self-efficacy" bias (Brown 1986; Hoorens 1993; Bandura 1982). People tend to inflate the degree to which they are more capable than those around them. While generally, self-efficacy allows people to have increased confidence in their ability and to achieve greater success with relatively low levels of emotional anxiety (Bandura 1982), self-efficacy bias has also been shown to increase one's dedication to "a losing course of action" (Whyte, Saks, and Hook 1997) and one's tendency to take greater risks (Krueger and Dickson 1995. That is, if one has a higher level of self-efficacy, they may commit to following a particular course of action for a longer period of time, even if it is doomed to fail.

While research on self-efficacy and computer use is limited, it primarily shows that students who have higher levels of self-efficacy regarding computer use are more likely to take computer courses (Hill et al. 1987), are more likely to use advanced technological products (Hill et al. 1987), and do well in software training (Gist et al. 1989); these studies are somewhat old and are from a time when computer use was less frequent among the general public. Our research shows that self-efficacy bias may lead students to take greater risks in online spaces, assuming that they are capable of preventing victimization.

4.2   Strategies Employed by Students to Overcome Risks

We found that students use several strategies to maintain their privacy and security in online spaces—some contradictory to technical risk assessment-based strategies recommended by cybersecurity professionals. Students rely heavily on source credibility and are more likely to trust websites they perceive as highly reputable, when engaging in activities such as Internet banking and online shopping. For instance, students state:

> Well, I do shop online, but it's from more, what I consider, big name reputable sites. If I can see if they have like a grade from the Better Business Bureau, I usually feel pretty safe.

> If I can actually just recognize their brand name right away, which sounds a little stupid, but it is pretty fair to say, because if I am going to go to eBay, and someone hacks into my account, they are going to have a lot of evidence, at least I hope they would. I feel like the more "big name" a site is, the more people use them, the less bad experience that I feel like have happened, per person, less likely it is going to happen to me. If it is like some shady site I have never heard of, I would rather meet with the people in real life, if it is like a real life store or something, or just avoid it.

Source credibility is an often-discussed topic in risk perception literature (Renn and Levin 1991; Fischhoff 1995). Credibility is, by extension, linked to trust and risk perception. Sources that are seen as more credible are also often seen as more trustworthy—leading to lower risk perceptions. In situations where credibility, trust, and risk are linked, users do not view information security as a priority (Bener 2000). For instance, speaking specifically on information systems, Bener (2000: p. 4) argues that users "perceive risks based on trust and credibility they assign to the supplier of information and disregard the security measures taken by that supplier."

A second strategy includes limiting what information students shared with others in online communities. As long as everything they publically shared was information they were comfortable with others having access to, students felt that they were not in any danger. This strategy specifically targets SNSs, and does not take into consideration other possible risky activities such as online purchases. For instance, typical student claims include:

> I personally don't feel at high risk of security online if I don't put anything I don't want people to know online.

Some students feel that actions required to stay safe on the Internet are too overwhelming, confusing, or futile. Because of this they avoid actively thinking about cybersecurity and fail to take steps to protect themselves online. For instance, one student, when prompted to discuss his concerns about cell phone hacking, expressed his belief that if someone wanted to hack into his phone, they would do so whether or not he took steps to protect the phone:

> Yeah so like I'm not gonna worry about something that I can't, that I don't have any control over.

This student also echoed these feelings when discussing security issues related to air traffic control. A second student, an accounting major, is also intimidated by cybersecurity. When discussing her feelings about government surveillance, she says:

> I try not to think about it, cause I know that's there, and you can't really do anything about it I guess. I know a lot of people who are super paranoid about it.

She continues on, expressing that paranoia regarding government surveillance would hinder her "ability to live her life." When discussing her concerns about SNSs, she continues in the same vein:

> I guess I think that there are a lot of risks with having your information out there, I can choose not to think about it, cause I can't control it.

Students who expressed similar sentiments seemed to regard themselves as unable to properly address security concerns. They were therefore overwhelmed to even think about cybersecurity. In many cases, this resulted in their not taking steps to stay safe on the internet, including avoidance of not only strategies that were complicated or required specialized knowledge, but also strategies that would be simple enough for them to understand and implement.

In this sense, student inaction seems to echo a variant of what social psychologists label "learned helplessness" (i.e., not attempting to overcome negative situations due to the belief that one has significantly less control over negative events) (Peterson and Seligman 1983). Contradictory to the general learned helplessness theory—which suggests that victimization increases emotional numbing and passivity in future responses to negative events—we found that even students who have not reported experiencing any negative Internet events, express lack of control and futility of action. We call this variant of learned helplessness "can-I-live syndrome"[1]—the idea that paying attention to, and taking action on, what is perceived as an overwhelming amount of online risks somehow reduces our overall quality of life.

5 Conclusion

Results of the current study show that, college student perceptions of cybersecurity are shaped predominantly by three phenomena: routinization and ritualization of risk, opti-

---

[1] "Can-I-Live" syndrome refers to an incident involving Hollywood reality star Kim Kardashian, where she cropped her daughter out of an Instagram photo for blinking during the selfie. When Kardashian became aware of the backlash to this act, she retorted, "Her eyes were closed and I was feeling my look! Can I live?!".

mistic bias, self-efficacy. Contrary to previous research (e.g., Lawyer et al. 2011), we did not find evidence to suggest that the lack of awareness of cyber threats/security was a major determinant of the overall risk experience of college students. Strategies employed by students to overcome online risks included accessing sources that they perceived as credible and trustworthy, restricting the amount of information shared with their online networks, and exercising learned helplessness.

Since the main issue, at least as far as Internet savvy college students are concerned, is not one of awareness, but one of routinization/ritualization of risk, we suggest that more awareness about risks may not be an effective solution to increase college students' online privacy and security. In fact, providing more information about risks may be counter-productive and lead to exacerbating the "can-I-live syndrome."

Alternatively, educational institutions such as colleges should focus on further automating protection within their cyber-networks. Educational programs should focus on steps that can be taken to protect one's security and privacy, rather than focusing on increasing awareness of online dangers. Further, they may find increased impacts if they focus on relatively simple tools that can provide significantly high benefits (e.g., antivirus software, firewalls, username and password security, encryption methods).

Mandatory changes that alter the context in which students behave and make decisions can also help. In this sense, we are advocating for institutional mandates/requirements that help develop "conscientious cybercitizens," defined by Anderson and Agarwal (2010) as "individuals who are motivated to take the necessary precautions under their direct control to secure their own computer and the Internet."

Acknowledgements. The authors would like to thank Michelle Sing for her research assistance and insightful comments. This research was partially supported through the University of Idaho IGEM Grant.

Appendix A: Semi-Structured Interview Guide

1. Did you have a computer growing up?
2. How much time did you spend online throughout your childhood?
3. What is the first thing that comes to mind when I say "cybersecurity"? (Follow-up: why?)
4. What activities do you do online? (social media, banking, gaming, gambling, skype, email, research, Bblearn, etc.)
5. What do you think are the greatest risks you face online? (Probe: privacy risks, government surveillance, corporate data collection, slander, etc.)
6. Why do you think that is the case?
7. Have you heard of any of the following?
   - Worms
   - Viruses
   - Trojan Horses
   - Malware
   - Phishing

     – Cyber bullying
     – Cyber stalking
     – Cell phone hacking/stalking

8. Of those you have heard of, can you define them?
9. To what degree are you concerned about each of these affecting you or your computer?
10. Have you ever been effected by any of these? If so, please tell me about that experience.
11. Do you know anyone who has been affected by these? If so, please tell me about their experience.
12. What percent of Internet users do you think are affected by these annually?
13. Are there activities you avoid doing because they are too risky in your eyes?
14. Do you do things you consider risky?
15. What sort of things make you trust the security of a site or online activity?
16. Do you log into public wi-fi networks freely? What concerns, if any, do you have in doing so?
17. If you are logged into a public wi-fi network, what sorts of activities do you engage in? What sorts of activities, if any, do you avoid?
18. Do you ever share your passwords? How do you make decisions about with whom you share passwords? What factors affect your decisions?
19. Do you install security software on your computer? What factors contribute to your decisions on this matter?
20. What, if any, are your concerns when downloading applications from the internet? How do you make decisions about what is safe to put on your computer?
21. How often do you change your passwords? What drives you to do this at the rate you do?
22. What sort of difficulties do you face when managing your security?
23. To what degree do you see the following as a potential threat online?
     – Corporate data collection (targeted ads, etc.)
     – Government (surveillance)
     – Hackers
     – Scammers
     – Terrorists
     – Debt collectors
     – Friends
     – Personal enemies
     – Stalkers
     – Peer groups
     – Others
24. Please explain your concerns.
25. Which social networking sites do you use? (If none, why not?)
26. What (if any) do you think are the biggest risks you face using these sites?
27. How much personal information do you feel comfortable sharing on these sites?

28. Have you ever had other people share information about you online, that you had thought was confidential? Please explain.
29. Have you ever had people online deceive you in some way? Please explain.
30. Do you have a smart phone? What sort of online activities do you do on your phone?
31. Have you heard of the following technologies?
    - Vehicle to vehicle communication
    - Vehicle to infrastructure communication
    - Smart houses
    - Smart phones
32. What, if any, are your security and privacy concerns regarding these technologies?
33. What benefits do you see from these projects?
34. How do you weigh the benefits against the risks?
35. To what degree do you see the threat of hacker attacks/security violations in the following areas:
    - Traffic lights
    - Air Traffic Control
    - Hospital/medical records
    - Power plants
    - Credit card data
36. What year are you in school?
37. What is your major?
38. In what region/town did you grow up?
39. With what race do you identify? (if say human, no answer, include perceived race)
40. With what gender do you identify?
41. What level education did your parents attain?
42. Approximately how much money do your parents make annually? What is their profession?
43. What is your religious affiliation?
44. With what political affiliation do you identify?

References

Al-Najjar, F., Al-Azemi, W., BuHaimed, W., Adib, S., Behbehani, J.: Knowledge and expectations among Kuwaiti mothers attending clinics for asthmatic children. Psychol. Health Med. 3(3), 253–259 (1998)

Anderson, C.L., Agarwal, R.: Practicing safe computing: a multimedia empirical examination of home computer user security behavioral intentions. MIS Q. 34(3), 613–643 (2010)

Ariely, D.: Our buggy moral code [Video file] (2009) http://www.ted.com/talks/dan_ariely_on_our_buggy_moral_code?language=en

Arnett, J.: Optimistic bias in adolescent and adult smokers. Addict. Behav. 25(4), 625–632 (2000)

Bandura, A.: Self-efficacy mechanism in human agency. Am. Psychol. 37(2), 122–147 (1982)

Beck, U.: Risk Society: Towards a New Modernity. Sage, London (1992)

Basar, B.A.: Credibility: a case in internet banking. Dissertation, London School of Economics and Political Science (2000)

Brown, J.D.: Evaluations of self and others: self-enhancement biases in social judgments. Social Cogn. **4**, 353–376 (1986)

Campbell, J., Greenauer, N., Macaluso, K., End, C.: Unrealistic optimism in internet events. Comput. Hum. Behav. **23**(2007), 1273–1284 (2007)

Chapin, J., Coleman, G.: Optimistic bias: what you think, what you know, or whom you know? North Am. J. Psychol. **11**(1), 121–132 (2009)

Debatin, B., Lovejoy, J.P., Horn, A.-K., Hughes, B.N.: Facebook and online privacy: attitudes, behaviors, and unintended consequences. J. Comput.-Mediated Commun. **15**(2009), 83–108 (2009)

Dilmac, B.: Psychological needs as a predictor of cyber bullying: a preliminary report on college students. Educ. Sci. Theory Pract. **9**(3), 1307–1325 (2009)

Ellison, N.B., Steinfield, C., Lampe, C.: The benefits of facebook "friends:" social capital and college students' use of online social network sites. J. Comput.-Mediated Commun. **12**(2007), 1143–1168 (2007)

Fischhoff, B.: Risk perception and communication unplugged: twenty years of process. Risk Anal. **15**(2), 137–145 (1995)

Fogel, J., Nehmad, E.: Internet social network communities: risk taking, trust, and privacy concerns. Comput. Hum. Behav. **25**, 153–160 (2009)

Frewer, L., Howard, C., Hedderley, D., Shepherd, R.: Methodological approaches to assessing risk perceptions associated with food-related hazards. Risk Anal. **18**(1), 95–102 (1998)

Giddens, A.: Risk and Responsibility. Mod. Law Rev. **62**(1), 1–10 (1999)

Gist, M.E., Schwoerer, C., Rosen, B.: Effects of alternative training methods on self-efficacy and performance in computer software training. J. Appl. Psychol. **74**, 884–891 (1989)

Helweg-Larsen, M., Shepperd, J.A.: Do moderators of the optimistic bias affect personal or target risk estimates? a review of the literature. Pers. Soc. Psychol. Rev. **5**, 74–95 (2001). doi: 10.1207/S15327957PSPR0501_5

Hill, T., Smith, N.D., Mann, M.F.: Role of efficacy expectations in predicting the decision to use advanced technologies. J. Appl. Psychol. **72**(1987), 307–314 (1987)

Hoorens, V.: Self-enhancement and superiority biases in social comparison. In: Strobe, W., Hewstone, M. (eds.) European Review of Social Psychology, pp. 113–139. Wiley, Chichester, UK (1993)

Ibrahim, Y.: The new risk communities: social networking sites and risk. Int. J. Media Cult. Polit. **4**(2), 245–253 (2008)

Jones, A., Ashenden, D.: Risk Management for Computer Security: Protecting Your Network and Information Assets. Butterworth-Heinemann, Oxford (2005)

Kendall, J.J.: Internet addiction on campus: the vulnerability of college students. CyberPsychol. Behav. **1**(1), 11–17 (1998)

Krueger, N.K., Dickson, P.R.: How believing in ourselves increases risk taking: perceived self-eYcacy and opportunity recognition. Decis. Sci. **25**, 385–400 (1995)

James, P.L., Molluzzo, J.C.: A survey of first-year college student perceptions of privacy in social networking. Consortium Comput. Sci. Coll. **26**(3), 36–41 (2011)

Lewis, K., Kaufman, J., Christakis, N.: The taste for privacy: an analysis of college student privacy settings in an online social network. J. Comput.-Mediated Commun. **14**(2008), 79–100 (2008)

Livingstone, S.: Taking risky opportunities in youthful content creation: teenagers' use of social networking sites for intimacy, privacy and self-expression. New Media Soc. **10**(3), 393–411 (2008)

Luo, J., Isaacowitz, D.: How optimists face skin cancer information: Risk assessment, attention, memory and behavior. Psychol. Health **22**(8), 963–984 (2007)

MacDonald, C.D., Roberts-Pittman, B.: Cyberbullying among college students: prevalence and demographic differences. Proc. Soc. Behav. Sci. **9**(2010), 2003–2009 (2010)

Mary, M., Rainie, L.: Pew research center 2015. Americans' Attitudes About Privacy, Security and Surveillance, 20 May 2015. (http://www.pewinternet.org/2015/05/20/americans-attitudes-about-privacy-security-and-surveillance/)

Morahan-Martin, J., Schumacher, P.: Loneliness and social use of the internet. Comput. Hum. Behav. **19**, 659–671 (2003)

Moreno, M.A., Stewart, M., Pumper, M., Cox, E., Young, H., Zhang, C., Eickhoff, J.: Facebook use during a stressful event: a pilot evaluation investigating facebook use patterns and biologic stress response. Bull. Sci. Technol. Soc. **34**(3–4), 94–98 (2014)

O'Keeffe, G.S., Clarke-Pearson, K.: The impact of social media on children, adolescents, and families. Pediatrics **127**(4), 800–804 (2011)

Peterson, C., Seligman, Martin E.P.: Learned helplessness and victimization. Soc. Issues (1983). doi:10.1111/j.1540-4560.1983.tb00143.x

Pew Research Center: Social networking fact sheet (2014), 21 May 2015. (http://www.pewinternet.org/fact-sheets/social-networking-fact-sheet/)

Ralson, P.A.S., Graham, J.H., Hieb, J.L.: Cybersecurity risk assessment for SCADA and DCS networks. ISA Trans. **46**(4), 583–594 (2007)

Ortwin, R., Levine, D.: Credibility and trust in risk communication. In: Kasperson, R.E., Stallen, P.J.M. (eds.) Communicating Risks to the Public, vol. 4, pp. 175–217. Springer, Heidelberg (1991)

Schenk, A.M., Fremouw, W.J.: Prevalence, psychological impact, and coping of cyberbully victims among college students. J. Sch. Violence **11**(1), 21–37 (2012)

Shibutani, T.: Reference groups as perspectives. Am. J. Sociol. **60**(6), 562–569 (1955)

Silverman, D.: Qualitative Methodology and Sociology. Gower Publishing, Aldershot, England (1985)

Tufekci, Z.: Can you see me now? audience and disclosure regulation in online social network sites. Bull. Sci. Technol. Soc. **28**(1), 20–36 (2008)

U.S. Chamber of Commerce Foundation: The Millennial Generation Research Review (2012), 20 May 2015 http://www.uschamberfoundation.org/millennial-generation-research-review

Valenzuela, S., Park, N., Kee, K.F.: Is there social capital in a social network site?: facebook use and college students' life satisfaction, trust, and participation. J. Comput.-Mediated Commun. **14**(2009), 875–901 (2009)

Walker, E., Caban, A., Schecter, C., Basch, C., Blanco, E., DeWitt, T., Kalten, M., Mera, M., Mojica, G.: Measuring comparative risk perceptions in an urban minority population. the risk perception survey for diabetes. Diab. Educ. **33**(1), 103–110 (2007)

Whyte, G., Saks, A., Hook, S.: When success breeds failure: the role of self-eycacy in escalating commitment to a losing course of action. J. Organ. Behav. **18**, 415–432 (1997)

How the Secure Use of Technology Could Influence Travel to and from School for Elementary School-Aged Children

Kevin Chang[✉], Kristin Haltinner, and Reilly Scott

University of Idaho, Moscow, ID, USA
chang@uidaho.edu

Abstract. A child's ability or opportunity to walk or bicycle to school is determined by his or her parents who must weigh a number of different factors in this decision. For this study, the concerns expressed by parents were evaluated along with exploring possible technological solutions that could be used to address these concerns and to guide policy decisions. Data were collected over a six-month period utilizing an online survey sent to parents of elementary school-aged children in Idaho. The findings suggest that parents' primary concerns regarding school safety included: distance to school, the possibility of a traffic and pedestrian accident, and child abduction by strangers. Parents were most comfortable with minimally to moderately invasive technological solutions including phone calls if students did not arrive in school, established checkpoints for students to pass en route to school, live streaming videos in the classroom, and GPS tracking of their child's backpack.

1 Introduction

Elementary school aged children have different options with regard to their mode of transport between their homes and their assigned schools but the variety used is limited. Walking or bicycling to school is the primary mode of travel only for children who live in a neighborhood or community where there are sidewalks and other infrastructure available; personal safety and security are afterthoughts, and there are limited crossing points where high traffic volumes or fast speeds are involved (Timperio, Ball, Salmon, Roberts, Giles-Corti, Simmons, Baur, and Crawford 2006; Schlossberg, Greene, Phillips, Johnson, and Parker 2006). Conversely, if the child physically lives a significant distance away from a school (typically outside of one mile), or if infrastructure and personal safety are perceived as lacking or of concern to a parent, the child will be dropped off and picked up by an adult or transported to and from the school by a school bus (McDonald 2008).

Walking and bicycling trends in the United States have significantly evolved over time. In 1969, 89 % of kindergarten to eighth grade (K-8) students who lived within one mile of school walked or bicycled to school. By 2009, only 35 % percent of these students who lived within one mile walked or bicycled to school even once a week (The National Center for Safe Routes to School 2011). This trend can be attributed to a number of different factors: an increase in dual-income parents who drive their children

© Springer International Publishing Switzerland 2016
K. Haltinner et al. (Eds.): CSS 2015, CCIS 589, pp. 82–104, 2016.
DOI: 10.1007/978-3-319-28313-5_7

to school as they simply do not have or make time to walk or bicycle with their children, increased concerns about child safety due to a corresponding increase in traffic volumes and speeds near schools; perceptions regarding personal safety and student abductions en route to school; and the siting of new schools on lower-cost land but which are no longer located in close proximity to neighborhoods and communities (The Safe Routes to School Online Guide 2015). These trends are highly correlated with a number of societal challenges including: higher fuel costs and bus transportation costs, increased traffic near schools, and missed opportunities for physical fitness in a time of increased childhood obesity.

In 2005, the United States Congress passed legislation that established a national program to improve safety on walking and bicycling to school and to encourage children and families to travel between home and school using these modes, and the National Safe Routes to School (SRTS) was signed into law in August 2005. As of 2012, this program has apportioned nearly $1.2 billion to various projects and programs and has provided a cumulative benefit to nearly 15,000 schools (Safe Routes National Center for Safe Routes to School 2015). The funding provided to these schools and the programs that have been developed show early promise; walking to and from school increased slightly between 2007 and 2012, from 12.4 % to 15.7 % in the morning and from 15.8 % to 19.7 % in the afternoon (Trends in Walking 2013).

The program and project solutions that promote good walking and bicycling habits are anecdotally referred to the "E's", namely: engineering, enforcement, education, encouragement, and occasionally evaluation (Safe Routes to School 2002). Engineering refers to infrastructure improvements; a robust walk or bicycle to school program must fundamentally have sidewalk and shoulder facilities that will allow a child's safe passage from home to school. Where resources are limited, prioritizing improvements based on school district walking routes or designated corridors may be necessary (Sundstrom, Pullen-Seufert, Cornog, Cynecki, and Chang 2010). Enforcement is provided by local police officers and sheriff deputies in the vicinity of schools and along walking routes. Their roles may range from targeting malicious behavior in the form of a speeding driver or jaywalker to simply having an active presence along these routes. Education is necessary to teach children and parents alike about the transportation choices that are available, and the benefits and consequences of each decision made. Encouragement refers to activities or events that promote a walking and bicycling alternative. Lastly, as projects and programs are implemented, evaluation is conducted and completed to assess outcome effectiveness. Although each individual component can provide a positive outcome, the collective application of these five E's serves as a more comprehensive approach to potentially affecting positive behavioral change.

2 Encouragement Opportunities

With regard to encouragement, the advancement of technology has opened the door to enabling parents to actively monitor their children as they walk or bicycle to school. By using the global positioning system (GPS) coordinates and the wireless fidelity with media access control address (wi-fi MAC address) of any connected device such as a mobile phone, bracelet, or watch, the location of that mobile object can be traced and tracked. This type of technology is used by transportation agencies such as rental car companies and transit agencies to monitor the locations of their fleet vehicles and to assess system performance.

Other systems require active interaction by the student in order to be tracked. For example, one programmable tracking system requires students to scan a card, and provides incentives to reinforce positive behavior when walking goals are met. The neighborhood school assigns a card to each student and notes the walking distance from each child's home to school; the student scans his or her card when he or she arrives at school in the morning. Each time a card is scanned the monitoring device tracks total miles traveled, as well as the total of number of trips made by the student. When the student reaches a certain mile threshold, he or she is eligible for a reward (Saris Cycling Group 2015).

Application software, or apps, are another way to encourage travel and enhance travel behavior. One example app designed for neighborhood parents by connecting them with other parents in their area to establish or collaborate walking school buses (Student Access Program 2015). A walking school bus is formed when two or more adults accompany a line of children and walk to school with them. The app that is used serves as a type of technology which is forward-thinking and represents a digital means to facilitate walking and biking to school. The app allows parents to search by elementary school for existing walking groups, create new groups and invite neighbors to join, plan walks to and from school, assign parent leaders to walk with students, and group text within the app. The app can also alert parents when students have arrived safely at school. Similar to the card-reading system, the app also has the capability of tracking the amount of trips taken by the student, total miles walked, emissions saved, and total calories burned. Other apps offer personal security services (Emergensee 2015).

As these technological advancements becomes more prevalent in our society, the genesis for this research project was to examine how the use of such technology could be used to alleviate some of the fears that parents have about child safety when their own son or daughter is walking or bicycling to school with limited or no parental supervision.

3 Methodology

In order to discover insights into the safety concerns of parents who have elementary school-aged children, a survey was developed to determine what factors affect parental decisions regarding a child's travel method. The role that encouragement measures have with regard to walking and bicycling to school were also examined to determine how this additional layer of information might influence child transportation to and from elementary schools.

Survey questions were developed based on previous literature on school transportation and safety (see Literature Review). Using this information a series of questions was developed for parents featuring the most common concerns and technology adaptations. This survey was then tested with a thirty-person pilot survey. This led to the improvement of existing questions and the development of additional factors to assess.

To disseminate the survey, an online questionnaire was created using Survey Monkey and sent via email to each elementary school principal throughout the State of Idaho. Email addresses for public school principals were collected from online sources. Principals who did not initially reply to the survey were contacted two additional times, three months apart.

In total, we were able to contact parents whose children attended schools in nineteen different districts in Idaho. A breakdown of the school districts is as follows: 21 % percent came from Blackfoot, 1 % from Boise, 2 % from Caldwell, 1 % from Challis, 2 % from Coeur d'Alene, 1 % from Dover, 1 % from Filer, 1 % from Genesee, two percent from Idaho Falls, five percent from Kuna, 24 % from Lewiston, two percent from Meridian, 13 % from Moscow, 7 % from Mountain Home, 1 % from Nampa, 1 % from Pocatello, 1 % from Rexburg, 11 % from Sandpoint, and 1 % rom Twin Falls.

Participants in our sample were parents with elementary school-aged children. We inquired as to basic demographic information of these parents and found that our sample had a higher income average than most Idahoans with only 7 % earning less than $25,000 a year, 12 % earning between $25,001 and $50,000, 24 % earning between $50,001 and $75,000, 37 % earning between $75,001 and $100,000, and 20 % earning more than $100,001 per year. Similarly, our sample seemed quite educated with 2 % having attended K-12 school but not graduating, 8 % having graduated college, 17 % having some college education but no degree, 3 % completing trade or technical training, 9 % completing an Associate's degree, 24 % having a Bachelor's degree, 30 % having a Master's degree, and 7 % having a Professional degree. No one in our sample had a PhD. Ninety-three percent of the sample were legally married or partnered, 2 % were single, 2 % were in long term committed partnerships, none were divorced, 1 % was separated and 1 % was widowed. In terms of political identity, 30 % of our sample identified as conservative, 21 % as moderately conservative, 27 % as moderate, 9 % as moderately liberal, and 13 % as liberal. Nearly all of the parents we surveyed were white: 95 %. One percent were Asian, 2 % were black or African American, 1 % identified as other, and no one identified as Native Hawaiian, Pacific Islander, American Indian, or Alaskan Native. Eighty-one percent of parents sampled were women, 19 % were men.

As is evident in Appendix A, the researchers asked parents to consider a single child of elementary school age while conducting the survey. Fifty-four percent of the respondents referred to their daughter while 46 % percent referred to their son throughout the survey. Forty-five percent of these children were the youngest child in the household, 31 % were the oldest, 17 % were a middle child, and 8 % were an only child. Four percent of these children were under the age of five, 9 % percent were six,

18 % were seven, 16 % were eight, 13 % were nine years old, 21 % were ten, 11 % were 11, three percent were 12 and 5 % were 13 or older. Ninety-nine percent of these children had no physical disability. Ninety-nine percent of children had no mental illness. Six percent did have a mental disability; this was self-disclosed by parents as their kids struggling with ADHD (Attention-Deficit/ Hyperactivity Disorder) in every case.

All information collected in this survey remained anonymous and confidential. There was no risk to school officials, parents, or to the children by participating in this survey. The information collected was only used to assess the decision-making process and develop models that measure how parents might select the home-to-school travel method for their children. Questions pertaining to a respondent's community type and environment, their children, and demographic data were asked. The survey introduction and questions are shown in Appendix A.

The data was then cleaned and entered into SPSS (Statistical Package for the Social Sciences). This software program was used to run descriptive statistics, Chi Squares, and logistic regression. These decisions were made based on the nature of the variables.

4   Results and Analysis

Our survey showed that, of the 143 students in question, 16 % walked or biked to school on their own some of the time, 8 % walked or biked with an adult, and 76 % did not walk or bike to school (N = 90). Participants were then asked specifically how their children traveled to school most often. Eight percent walked or biked on their own, 5 % walked or biked with an adult, 0 % walked or biked with other children, 34 % rode the bus, 4 % carpooled, and 40 % were driven alone by a caretaker (N = 91).

4.1   The First Wave of Red Flags

After developing this baseline information, participants were asked about the primary factors that contribute to a parent's comfort level when their children walk to school: distance to school, the presence of sidewalks, and the presence of crossing guards (Timperio et al. 2006). In our sample, 63 % of the families live farther than one mile from the school, 13 % live approximately one mile from the school, 9 % percent live three quarters of a mile from the school, 6 % live half a mile away and 9 % live within one quarter mile from the school (N = 91).

Regarding coverage of sidewalks, 28 % of parents reported that there were sidewalks on the route to school, 47 % said there were not, and 25 % indicated that there was some coverage (N = 90). Considering the presence of crossing guards, 13 % said that there were crossing guards along the route, 27 % said their were not, and 60 % said there was some crossing guard coverage (N = 91).

Another factor that may contribute to one's transportation decision is the length of time a student's bus trip would take. In our sample, 33 % said the trip took less than 15 min, 36 % said it took between 16–30 min, 21 % said it lasted 31–45 min, 5 % reported the ride taking 46–60 min and 4 % said the trip was longer than an hour (N = 81).

4.2   The Concerns of Parents

After establishing an understanding of how some of the most common concerns apply to our sample, parents were asked about their primary fears regarding their children walking or biking to school.

We first asked parents the degree to which the following concerns affected their decision: physical harm by others, proximity to high traffic areas, and child safety on the bus. Thirty-five percent reported the fear of physical harm by others affected their decision to a large extent, 22 % to a moderate extent, 18 % to some extent, 14 % to a little extent, and 11 % said it did not affect their decision at all (N = 89). Regarding proximity to high traffic areas, 60 % of parents said this affected their decision to a large extent, 20 % to a moderate extent, 9 % to some extent, 5 % to a little extent, and 5 % said it didn't effect their decision at all (N = 89). Finally, regarding bus safety, 18 % said this contributed to their decision to a large extent, 17 % to a moderate extent, 15 % to some extent, 21 % to a little extent, and 29 % not at all (N = 89) (Table 1).

Table 1. Parents level of concern for primary fears

Fear	To a large extent	To a moderate extent	To some extent	To a little extent	Not at all
Physical harm by others?	35 %	22 %	18 %	14 %	11 %
Proximity to high traffic Areas?	60 %	20 %	9 %	5 %	5 %
Bus safety?	18 %	17 %	15 %	21 %	29 %

Parents were then asked to rank their fears from most significant to the one that had no influence (see Table 2). Please note: they could select more than one option as having the most significance. Forty-one percent said distance to school was the most significant factor. This was followed by kidnapping or abduction by a stranger (23 %), traffic or car accidents (22 %), other crime (9 %), kidnapping or abduction by a family member (8 %), bullying (7 %), their child getting lost en route (4 %), their child getting distracted en route (2 %), or their child skipping school (1 %). Parents ranked traffic and car accidents as a significant factor (35 %), followed by distance to school (26 %), kidnapping and abduction by a stranger (24 %), children getting lost en route (18 %), bullying (10 %), children getting distracted (9 %), kidnapping or abduction by a family member (8 %), other crime (6 %), and children skipping school (5 %). Parents reported other crime as the most common factor having some influence (18 %) followed by traffic and car accidents and kidnapping or abduction by a stranger (17 %), distance to school (14 %), bullying (13 %), children getting lost en route (10 %), kidnapping or abduction by a stranger (8 %), children getting distracted (3 %), and their children skipping school (2 %). Parents reported other crime as the most likely to have a minor influence (27 %) followed by bullying (26 %), children getting lost en route (21 %), kidnapping or abduction by a stranger (17 %), traffic and car accidents (16 %), children getting distracted (13 %), kidnapping or abduction by a family member (11 %), distance to school (8 %), and children skipping school (7 %). Parents reported their children skipping school as the most likely factor to have no influence over their decisions (66 %), followed by children getting distracted (53 %), kidnapping or abduction by a family member (48 %), children getting lost en route (32 %), bullying (30 %), other crime (26 %), kidnapping or abduction by a stranger (10 %), distance to school (7 %), and traffic or car accidents (5 %). Finally, parents reported their children getting distracted as the factor that was most likely not a concern (22 %), followed by children skipping school (19 %), kidnapping or abduction by a family member (17 %), children getting lost en route and other crime (15 %), bullying (13 %), kidnapping or abduction by a stranger (9 %), traffic or car accidents (7 %), and distance to school (5 %).

Table 2. Parents fears ranked (N = 89)

Ranked fears	Distance to school	Traffic/car accidents	Kidnapping/ abduction by family member	Kidnapping/ abduction by stranger	Children skipping school	Children getting lost en route	Children getting distracted	Bullying	Other crime
Most significant	41 %	22 %	8 %	23 %	1 %	4 %	2 %	7 %	9 %
Significant	26 %	34 %	8 %	24 %	5 %	18 %	9 %	10 %	6 %
Some influence	14 %	17 %	8 %	17 %	2 %	10 %	3 %	13 %	18 %
Minor influence	8 %	16 %	11 %	17 %	7 %	21 %	13 %	26 %	27 %
No influence	7 %	5 %	48 %	10 %	66 %	32 %	53 %	30 %	26 %
Not a concern	5 %	7 %	17 %	9 %	19 %	15 %	22 %	13 %	15 %

Next, parents were asked what technology could be used to help them feel safe allowing their children to walk to school (N = 87). They were also asked if they would consider adopting each technology (N = 86) and whether or not they felt each technology was unethical (N = 79) (see Table 3). Eighty percent of parents said that receiving a phone call from the school if their child didn't arrive would make them feel secure, 78 % said they would consider adopting it, and 3 % said they felt this was an unethical measure. Eighteen percent of parents said that having established checkpoints for children to pass through en route to school would make them feel secure, 23 % said they would consider adopting this, and 1 % said they felt this was unethical. Twenty percent of parents said they would feel secure if they were able to remotely access a live stream video of their children's classroom, 23 % said they would consider adopting this technology, and 32 % considered this measure unethical. Thirty-seven percent of parents said that having a GPS tracker in their child's backpack would help them feel secure, 42 % said they would consider adopting this technology, and 17 % said they believed this measure to be unethical. Finally, 6 % of parents reported that placing biometric implants (microchips) in their children would make them feel secure, 5 % said they would consider adopting this technology, and 96 % felt this measure was unethical. Additionally 13 % said they would not use any of these technologies: 8 % because they felt secure and 5 % because they had ethical issues with them.

Table 3. Safety measures and parental comfort

	Phone call if no show	Established checkpoints	Live stream video in class	GPS tracking of backpack	Biometric implants
Feel secure?	80 %	18 %	20 %	37 %	6 %
Would consider adopting?	78 %	23 %	23 %	42 %	5 %
Unethical?	3 %	1 %	32 %	17 %	96 %

It is clear from this data that most parents would feel secure with and comfortable adopting minimally invasive technology (a phone call if their child doesn't arrive at school), but are uncomfortable with measures such as microchips.

5 Discussion and Conclusion

Using this data, we completed a series of logarithmic regression analyses in order to understand the relationship between demographic factors, parental fears, and the solutions they feel most comfortable adapting. We first compared demographic factors and transportation method selected. We found no correlation between gender of child, age of child, nor birth order of child and transportation method. Contrary to other scholars, we also found an absent relationship between the presence of sidewalks or crossing guards and transportation method. However, we did find that distance to school was a factor in the transportation method employed: the greater the distance, the less likely a child would walk or bike to school. This has also been confirmed by other researchers on this subject (Schlossberg, Greene, Phillips, Johnson, and Parker 2006).

We also examined the relationship between parental fears and the technology they preferred to adopt. We found that parents who fear kidnapping by stranger are more likely to be willing to adopt live streaming video in the classroom (p = 0.003). We also found that these parents (who fear kidnapping by stranger) are more likely to be willing to adopt putting a GPS tracker in their child's backpack (p = 0.003). Additionally, parents who fear their child will get lost on the way to school are more willing to adopt checkpoints on the way to school (p = 0.003). Finally, parents who fear their child will skip school are more likely to refuse adopting any option (p = 0.004), as are people who fear other crime (p = 0.006). These findings appear logical as it would seem that people with more severe fears would be willing to take more dire measures to protect their child (Ungar 2009). It also follows that parents who fear their children would get lost would approve of a system that would help them navigate their path to school.

Comparing demographic information to fears, we found that parents with higher levels of education are more likely to fear traffic/car accidents. We also found that parents with higher levels of education are more likely to fear their child will get lost en route to school. This may reflect previous findings by scholars that parents with greater levels of education are more likely to have authoritarian parenting styles (Hoff, Laursen, and Tardif 2002).

It is also important to note that we did not find several correlations that we expected to. First, there was no correlation between comfort with technology and adoption preference. There was also no correlation between town size and adoption preference. Finally, there was no correlation between political ideology and adoption preference. This could be a result of our sample size; having a larger number of participants would afford greater statistical analysis. It may also be a result of our location: Idaho, in which there are few self-reported progressives.

Our survey helps shine light on how parents may process the encouragement factors outlined by the Safe Routes to School Program. While the policy suggests the use of biometric chips, this seems a factor that parents are wholly resistant to. Another suggestion made by the organization is tracking via card, this could be similar to GPS tracking of a backpack. We find greater support and fewer ethical concerns for the use of this technology. Finally, while not a suggestion made by Safe Routes, we find that a number of parents may feel more comfortable allowing their children to walk to school if they knew they would be contacted if the student failed to show. While many school districts already employ this measure, it may be the case that parents are unaware of this service.

To extend this research we plan to use this data and the newer developments in suggestions from organizations such as Safe Routes to School to improve our surveys. We also plan to expand our data set to the parents of other states in the Pacific Northwest and Inland Pacific including Washington, Oregon, and Montana.

Acknowledgements. This research was partially supported with funding from the University of Idaho's Center for Secure and Dependable Systems through the Idaho Global Entrepreneurial Mission.

Appendix A: Survey

Transportation and Student Safety Survey Information

Over the past several decades there has been a dramatic decrease in the number of children who walk or bicycle to school. This survey is intended to provide insight into the safety concerns of parents who have elementary school-aged children and to determine what factors affect decisions regarding their child's travel method. We also seek to understand how technology might influence a parent's decision to allow their children to walk or bicycle to school.

All information collected in this survey will remain anonymous and confidential. There is no risk to you for participating in this survey and the information collected will only be used to assess the decision-making process and develop models that measure how parents might select the home-to-school travel method for their children.

Thank you for participating in this project. If you have any questions or comments please contact the primary investigators: Dr. Kristin Haltinner (khaltinner@uidaho.edu) or Dr. Kevin Chang (kchang@uidaho.edu).

(You may keep this for your records.)

The first series of questions ask about the community in which you live and your comfort level with technology.

1. How large is the town in which you live?

Less than 5,000 residents   50,000-100,000 residents

5,001-10,000 residents   Over 100,000 residents

10,001-50,000 residents

2. How long have you lived in your current community/neighborhood?

Less than one year   11-15 years

1-5 years   16-20 years

6-10 years   Longer than 20 years

3. How large is the town/city in which you were (primarily) raised?

Less than 5,000 residents   50,000-100,000 residents

5,001-10,000 residents   Over 100,000 residents

10,001-50,000 residents   Other (please specify):

4. On a scale of 1–5, how comfortable are you with using new technologies?

1 (Very uncomfortable)   4 (Somewhat comfortable)

2 (Somewhat uncomfortable)   5 (Very comfortable)

3 (Neutral)   Other (please specify):

The next series of questions focus on your feelings towards child safety and school transportation. While answering these questions consider ONE of your elementary school-aged children.

5. What age is this child?

5 or under

6	10
7	11
8	12
9	13 or older

6. In what place in the birth order does this child fall?
Oldest

Somewhere in the middle

Youngest

Only child

7. What is the child's gender?
Male

Female

Other (please specify):

8. Is your child physically disabled?
Yes

No

Unknown

If yes or unknown, please explain:

9. Does your child have a mental illnesses?

Yes

No

Unknown

If yes or unknown, please describe:

10. Does your child have a mental disability?

Yes

No

Unknown

If yes or unknown, please describe:

For these questions please continue considering the same child for which you answered questions on the previous page.

11. What is the approximate distance in miles from your household to your child's school?

0.25 or less

0.5 miles

0.75 miles

1 mile

More than 1 mile

12. Does this child walk or bike to school?

Yes, On His/Her Own

Yes, But Only With Adult Supervision

No

13. What is the primary method by which your child is transported to school?

They walk or bike on their own

They walk or bike with a group of children

They walk or bike with an adult

They take the bus

They are driven in a car pool

They are driven exclusively by family members

Other (please specify):

14. Are there sidewalks along the route to school?
Yes

Some Sidewalks/Partial Coverage

No

15. Are there crossing guards present at the intersections along the route to school?
Yes

Some Crossing Guards/Partial Coverage

No

16. How long would the child's commute to school take if they rode the bus?

Less than 15 minutes

16-30 minutes

31-45 minutes

46-60 minutes

More than an hour

Other (please specify):

17. To what extent does fear of physical harm by others shape your decision to allow your child to walk or bicycle to school?

To a large extent

To a moderate extent

To some extent

To a little extent

Not at all

18. To what extent does close proximity to high traffic areas or busy intersections influence your decision to allow your child to walk to school?

To a large extent   To a lit tle extent

To a moderate extent   Not at all

To some extent

19. To what extent does concern for your child's safety on the bus affect your decisions regarding transportation to school?

To a large extent   To a little extent

To a moderate extent   Not at all

To some extent

20. If it is geographically possible for your child to walk to school, but they do not, what factors contribute to this decision?

21. Please rank the following options by the extent to which they play a factor in your decision regarding whether or not your children walks or bikes to school:

	This is the most significant factor.	This factor has significant influence.	This factor has some influence.	This factor has minor influence.	This factor has no influence.	I am not concerned about my children walking or bicycling to school
Distance to school	5	4	3	2	1	0
Traffic/car accidents	5	4	3	2	1	0

Kidnapping/ abduction by family or friend	5	4	3	2	1	0
Kidnapping/ abduction by stranger	5	4	3	2	1	0
Children skipping school by their own will or peer pressure	5	4	3	2	1	0
Children getting lost on their way to school	5	4	3	2	1	0
Students getting distracted and forgetting to go to school	5	4	3	2	1	0
Bullying by other students	5	4	3	2	1	0
Other crime in the community	5	4	3	2	1	0

22. Which of these methods of tracking your child's arrival to school would make you feel most secure as a parent? (mark all that apply)

Receive a phone call/email if child fails to arrive

Established checkpoints determine if child is en route to school

Available live stream video feed for you to see if child is in class

GPS tracking of child's phone or backpack

Biometric implants (microchips under their skin) that would track child's progress to school

None of these: I am presently comfortable with my child walking to school

None of these: I have ethical issues with these options

Other (please specify)

23. Which of these methods of tracking your children's arrival to school would you consider adopting? (mark all that apply)

Receive a phone call/email if child fails to arrive

Established checkpoints determine if child is en route to school

Available live stream video feed for you to see if child is in class

GPS tracking of child's phone or backpack

Biometric implants (microchips under their skin) that would track child's progress to school

None of these: I am presently comfortable with my child walking to school

None of these: I have ethical issues with these options

Other (please specify)

24. Please rank these items in terms of the degree to which you would like to use them to track your child's progress to school:

Receive a phone call/email if child fails to arrive	First	Second	Third	Fourth	Fifth	N/A
Established checkpoints determine if child is en route to school	First	Second	Third	Fourth	Fifth	N/A
Available live stream video feed for you to see if child is in class	First	Second	Third	Fourth	Fifth	N/A
GPS tracking of child's phone or backpack	First	Second	Third	Fourth	Fifth	N/A
Biometric implants (microchips under their skin) that would track child's progress to school	First	Second	Third	Fourth	Fifth	N/A

Other (please specify):

25. Do you feel that any of the following methods of tracking your child's progress to school would be unethical? (Mark all that apply)

Receive a phone call/email if child fails to arrive

Established checkpoints determine if child is en route to school

Available live stream video feed for you to see if child is in class

GPS tracking of child's phone or backpack

Biometric implants (microchips under their skin) that would track child's progress to school

Optional: please explain your answer

26. What else would you like us to know about your feelings regarding security, safety, and your child's transportation to school?

These next questions collect additional demographic data so that we can look for patterns or trends in peoples' answers.

Less than $25,000	$75,001-$100,000
$25,001-$50,000	$100,001 or more
$50,001-$75,000	

27. What is the expected annual income for your household?
28. What is the highest degree or level of school you have completed? (If currently

Some K-12 school, no high school diploma	Bachelor's degree
or GED	
High school graduate or GED	Master's degree
Some college, no degree	Professional degree
Trade/Technical/Vocational training	Doctorate degree
Associate degree	

enrolled, select the highest degree received)

29. If married or partnered, what is the highest degree or level of school completed by your spouse/partner?

Some K-12 school, no high school diploma   Some high school, no diploma

or GED   High school graduate, diploma or GED

Some college, no degree   Master's degree

Trade/Technical/Vocational training   Professional degree

Associate degree   Doctorate degree

Bachelor's degree

Single   Separated

In a Long Term Committed Partnership   Widowed

Married/Legally Partnered   Other (please specify):

Divorced

30. What is your current marital status?

31. If Divorced or Separated, do you share custody?

Yes

No

N/A

32. How many adults in your household are currently employed including yourself?

0

1

2

3 or more

33. What political ideology do you affiliate with?

Conservative

Moderately Conservative

Moderate

Moderately Liberal

Liberal

34. What political party most closely aligns with your views?

Tea Party

Libertarian Party

Republican Party

Democratic Party

Green Party

Other (please specify):

35. Which racial category do you identify with? (Select all that apply)

American Indian or Alaska Native

Asian

Black or African American

Native Hawaiian or Other Pacific Islander

White

Other (please specify):

36. Are you Hispanic or Latino/a? (A person of Cuban, Mexican, Puerto Rican, South or Central American, or other Spanish Culture or Origin, Regardless of Race.)

Yes

No

37. What is your gender?

Male

Female

Other (please specify):

38. Were you born in the United States? (If "no", please include your country of origin.)

Yes

No (please specify):

39. What is your zip code? (This will not be used in any reporting, it is simply to help us organize data.)

Answer the following demographic questions for a secondary decision maker (if applicable), regarding how you child is transported to school.

40. How is this person related to your child?
Father

Mother

Step Father

Step Mother

Grandparent

Older Sibling

The Child Him/Herself

Other (please specify

41. What is the highest degree or level of school this individual has completed? (If currently enrolled, select the highest degree received)

Some K-12, no high school diploma or GED	Bachelor's degree
High school graduate or GED	Master's degree
Some college, no degree	Professional degree
Trade/Technical/Vocational training	Doctorate degree
Associate degree	

42. What racial category does this individual identify with? (Select all that apply)

American Indian or Alaska Native	Native Hawaiian or Other Pacific Islander
Asian	White
Black or African American	Other (please specify):

43. Is this individual Hispanic or Latino/a? (A person of Cuban, Mexican, Puerto Rican, South or Central American, or other Spanish Culture or Origin, Regardless of Race.)
Yes

No

44. What is this individual's gender?
Male

Female

Other (please specify):

45. Was this individual born in the United States? (If "no", please include country of origin.)
Yes

No (please specify):

References

Emergensee (2015). https://emergensee.com/. Accessed on 30 September 2015. https://emergensee.com/

Hoff, E., Laursen, B., Tardif, T.: Socieconomic status and parenting. In: Bornstein, M.H. (ed.) Handbook of Parenting, vol. 2, pp. 231–252. Lawrence Erlbaum Associates, Mahwah (2002)

McDonald, N.: Children's mode choice for the school trip: the role of distance and school location in walking to school. Transportation **35**, 23–35 (2008)

National Center for Safe Routes to School, How children get to school: school travel patterns from 1969 to 2009 (2011). Accessed on 25 September 2015. http://saferoutesinfo.org/sites/default/files/resources/NHTS_school_travel_report_2011_0.pdf

Safe Routes to School, United States Department of Transportation, National Highway Traffic Safety Administration, HS 809 497 (2002)

Safe Routes National Center for Safe Routes to School, 2015, History of SRTS. Accessed on 25 September 2015. http://www.saferoutesinfo.org/about-us/history-srts

Safe Routes to School Online Guide. 2015. The decline of walking and bicycling. Accessed on 25 September 2015. http://guide.saferoutesinfo.org/introduction/the_decline_of_walking_and_bicycling.cfm

Saris Cycling Group, 2015. What is The Hub? Accessed on 23 September 2015. https://thehub.saris.com/TheHub/learn.aspx

Schlossberg, M., Green, J., Phillips, P.P., Johnson, B., Parker, B.: School Trips: Effects of Urban Form and Distance on Travel Mode. J. Am. Plann. **72**(3), 337–346 (2006)

Student Neighborhood Access Program, (SNAP). 2015. Walking School Bus App. Utah Department of Transportation. http://www.udot.utah.gov/snap/CommonAccess/Walking_School_Bus_App.php?id=32. Accessed 23 September 2015

Sundstrom, C., Pullen-Seufert, N., Cornog, M., Cynecki, M., Chang, K.: Prioritizing schools for safe routes to school infrastructure projects. ITE J. **80**(2), 24–28 (2010)

Trends in walking and bicycling to school: takeaways for building successful programs, National Center for Safe Routes to School (2013). http://www.saferoutesinfo.org/sites/default/files/Trends_in%20Walking_and_Bicycling_to_School-Takeaways_for_Building_Successful_Programs.pdf

Ungar, M.: Overprotective parenting: helping parents provide children the right amount of risk and responsibility. Am. J. Fam. Therapy **37**(3), 258–271 (2009)

System and Process Assessments for Improved Cybersecurity

An Assessment Model and Methodology for National Security Systems

Jennifer Guild[(✉)]

Department of the Navy,
Naval Facilities Engineering Command,
Poulsbo, USA
jennifer.guild@gmail.com

Abstract. All computer systems or systems of computers are composed of some combination of three basic components; hardware, firmware, and software. These systems are assessed to determine the assessor's and the risk acceptor's confidence in their level of robustness, where robustness is the characterization of strength of a security function, mechanism, service, or solution, and the assurance that it is implemented and that it is functioning correctly. Most experienced assessors are aware that the level of robustness required for each system is dependent upon dynamic factors such as operational environment, threat source interest, and mission criticality. This paper will provide mathematical models of these factors and an assessment methodology that builds upon those models.

1 Background

Most people automatically assume the strength of the security capabilities of a computer system, heretofore referred to as system, based upon their knowledge, experience, cultural background, and the association of that system to its functionality. The average United States (U.S.) metropolitan citizen is confident their bank has significantly stronger security measures in place than the free wireless at the local Starbucks. That characterization of the strength of a security service and the confidence that it is implemented and functioning correctly is referred to as robustness. A security service is a capability that supports one or more security requirements (confidentiality[1], integrity[2], availability[3]), with one example being authentication[4] [1].

---

[1] Per CNSS 4009 confidentiality is the property that information is not disclosed to system entities (users, processes, devices) unless they have been authorized to access the information.

[2] Per CNSS 4009 integrity is the property whereby an entity has not been modified in an unauthorized manner.

[3] Per CNSS 4009 availability is the property of being accessible and useable upon demand by an authorized entity.

[4] Per CNSS 4009, authentication is the process of verifying the identity or other attributes claimed by or assumed of an entity (user, process, or device), or to verify the source and integrity of data.

© Springer International Publishing Switzerland 2016
K. Haltinner et al. (Eds.): CSS 2015, CCIS 589, pp. 107–126, 2016.
DOI: 10.1007/978-3-319-28313-5_8

There are certain systems, such as the federal banking system and National Security Systems[5] (NSS) [1] that require a greater level of robustness so as to not allow an unauthorized person or system to access the system being protected. Such access could result in damage to our financial markets (e.g., stock market crash due to "software glitch" in 2012) [2], federal banks being unable to conduct day-to-day business (e.g., cyber attack on Georgian banks in 2008) [3], or power grids going black (e.g., transformer failure causes failure of key computer in 2012) [4].

As technology progresses, so does our understanding of systems. A system is no longer just a desktop computer, but includes mobile devices (such as mobile phones, tablets, and wearable devices), newer automobiles that have embedded Bluetooth, GPS, cellular technologies, and commercial aircraft systems. Whether the system is a vehicle, mobile phone, or a laptop, if it is to be implemented by or connected to the U.S. Government (USG) systems, its level of robustness and assurance must be assessed.

A robustness or assurance assessment is a process or methodology in which system artifacts are identified, collected as evidence, and assessed against a single implementation of a system (referred to as a model), to determine the level of risk to USG by the implementation or operation of this system. Assessors must consider that the level of robustness required for each system is dependent upon dynamic factors, including but not limited to, operational environment (reflects the physical characterization of the environment), threat source interest, and mission criticality.

Assessors provide findings, aka evidence, to Authorizing Officials (AO), who then accept the risk of implementing the system. In current USG system assessment methodologies, the assessment is composed of two testing events. First, the technical testing is conducted on a lab-based system implementation. Following that test event, testing is conducted on the system as it is implemented in an operational (live) environment.

This composition, or lack of decomposition, is very important because the assessment approach, evidence, and results have the operational requirements, vulnerabilities, constraints, countermeasures, and threat assessments of that single implementation imposed onto all subsequent implementers, which hinders reciprocity[6].

---

[5] Per CNSSI 4009: Any information system (including any telecommunications system) used or operated by an agency or by a contractor of any agency, or other organization on behalf of an agency, the function, operation, or use of which: I. involves intelligence activities; II. involves cryptologic activities related to national security; III. Involves command and control of military forces; IV. involves equipment that is an integral part of a weapon or weapon system; or V. subject to subparagraph (B), is critical to the direct fulfillment of military or intelligence missions; or is protected at all times by procedures established for information that have been specifically authorized under criteria established by an Executive Order or an Act of Congress to be kept classified in the interest of national defense or foreign policy. (B). Does not include a system that is to be used for routine administrative and business applications (including payroll, finance, logistics, and personnel management applications). (Title 44 U.S. Code Sect. 3542, Federal Information Security Management Act of 2002).

[6] Reciprocity is the mutual recognition of the validity of the robustness and risk among a community, in this case the community is the US Department of Defense (DoD), US Intelligence Community (IC), and remainder of the USG.

Threats, vulnerabilities, risk, and impact must be considered at the conceptual design stage to increase assurance of a system. An independent Information System Security Engineer (ISSE) that is involved in the system development processes starting at design conception, can increase the measure of confidence in the assurance of the system by identifying applicable supplementary artifacts, and through the use of subject matter expertise, increase the quality of all assurance evidence.

An ISSE does not imply any theoretical background, because many ISSEs, as well as the AOs have learned to assess systems and risk while doing just that. An ISSE or AO that has a theoretical education or background in Computer Science (CS), Computer Engineering (CE), Electrical Engineering (EE), or Mathematics is unusual. That key aspect of having an experienced workforce with extremely varied exposure is a primary driver for creating an easily understood and implementable assessment methodology that integrates an objective mathematical model.

In previous and current assessment methodologies, the assessor's were and are delivered completed products. An argument has been made that assessing a completed product does not achieve the stated robustness level. Therefore, sufficient insight and engagement during the development lifecycle, which provides confidence that the system operates as it should, couldn't/cannot be achieved. The level of detail transferred between assessors, as well as assessors to AOs is based on assessor's experience, etc. This information, combined with the widely varied backgrounds and education of ISSEs, assessors, and AOs, provides further evidence of a key gap in existing assessment methodologies. That gap is a primary driver for creating an easily understand and implementable assessment methodology that implements an objective mathematical model.

As such, there is an opportunity to provide an assessment methodology, which includes mathematical models, for all technical and/or operational environments that can be combined with the current and future assessment methodologies, improve confidence in the system by requiring an independent assessor to integrate into the development process to achieve greater insight, and improve cost savings by preventing duplicate assessments and reducing time it takes to conduct assessments by allowing future assessments to build on the findings of past assessments. Both of which occur as a direct result of the implementation of the models within this methodology.

2 Assessment Methodology

In all assessments, evidence must be collected and assessed against a model. In existing assessment methodologies, that model is a live, single implementation of a system in a specific operational environment. The models presented support existing methodologies as guides to assessors to use for system design and development, security controls tailoring, and risk determinations. Those same models provide a basis for a new assessment methodology that is complementary to existing methodologies and can be used for either or both technical and operational assessments. For a technical assessment, the methodology is conducted by an independent security engineer as an assessor as the system is designed and developed, thereby completing that assessment when the system has completed development and prior to implementation at any operational environment. The methodology can also be used for an operational environment assessment of a system as it is implemented within that site.

The methodology can be implemented at any time within the development lifecycle of a system. The earlier in the lifecycle the methodology is implemented, the more it increases the evidence, such as documents, diagrams, mathematical proofs, testing, and ISSE's notes of each component of the system and the overall, available to the assessor. In addition, it strongly integrates the assessor with the system's developers and engineers, which provides expertise and critical information to assessor as the system is developed. Currently, the majority of systems do not have an ISSE involved throughout lifecycle of the system, if at all. Thus, assessors and decision makers must rely on documents and designs provided by the vendor, which are biased to provide the assurance specified by the vendor. Testing of a system and its components, however, can only provide assurance regarding the exploits being exercised against known vulnerabilities.

The methodology provides the assessors with the mechanisms to map the evidence to mathematical models in order to represent assessor's assessment findings, thereby providing consistency of assessor's findings. The use of the models increases objectiveness/explicitness, repeatability, and knowledge of system robustness from assessor to risk acceptor, as well as from assessor to assessor. The methodology will increase system reuse, reciprocity, and risk acceptance while decreasing the amount of time for subsequent assessments. In both methodologies, the individual models will be iteratively developed, fulfilling the needs of the assessor to represent their initial impression of the system's capabilities, represent the system's capabilities as it is assessed, and finally, to representatively correlate or map the completed models to the empirical evidence of the assessment.

The models must be simple enough for non-computer scientists or non-mathematicians to utilize and understand. That accommodation will increase their use among all assessors and the diminished complexity will increase the consistency of their implementation. The models may be implemented in any methodology.

Within the methodology, there are multiple stages with each stage correlating to the progression of the assessor's exposure to the system. Key stages include:

- Initial contact providing very basic overview of the system and its requirements
- Initial document review providing more insight to the system
- System familiarization
- System pre-assessment
- Assessment
- Data correlation.

At each stage, the assessor iterates the individual models to represent their impression of the system's capabilities. As the assessor's knowledge of the system increases, the content of these models will go from generalized to specific as the assessment progresses. At each stage, the assessor correlates the models to the evidence available to them at that stage. This methodology will provide a level of assessment detail previously not provided.

The methodology provides the ability to model system states to characterize dynamic aspects. The first computer was aptly named the Turing State Machine.

Computers alter states every time a binary decision is completed. So, computers and networks exist in fluidity, each constantly changing. However, the current common practice is to assess a single state, the state at which the system exists at the time of assessment. The models need to represent system in multiple states based on dynamic aspects, analogous to the modeling used in forecast models, nuclear explosions, and disease infection rates. This type of modeling has not previously been applied to system's security aspects, and would provide the advantage of the objective evidence throughout the assessment.

3   Assessment Models

There are a number of aspects an assessor must consider when assessing a system, regardless of its complexity or connectivity. An assessment is rarely a single, continuous event. As the assessment process progresses, assessor's knowledge of the system increases and the content of these models will go from generalized to specific.

Instead of an a priori risk determination, operational risk should be determined by the operational assessors of the system based primarily upon the technical risk derived from a technical assessment and further characterized by their operational assessment. Currently, a vulnerability assessment, as defined by CNSSI 4009, is the systematic examination of an information system or product to determine the adequacy of security measures, identify security deficiencies, provide data from which the effectiveness of the proposed security measures can be predicted, and confirm the adequacy of such measures after implementation [1].

The operational environment is more than just a fixed, land based operational environment, such as a workstation or Network Operations Center (NOC). A specific operational environment is a situational instance or state, which reflects a physical characterization of the operational environments (such as an aircraft in flight vs an aircraft parked on the deck of a carrier). Each situational instance/state will be individually modeled for countermeasures, vulnerabilities, threats, probabilities, attack vectors, impacts, risk, and effects to greatly improve the conciseness and objectivity of evidence for assessment, to provide increased reciprocation among assessors, and justification of effort (cost, etc.) for design and assessment of systems.

These categories are broad and generalized. A more specific detailing will define a situational instance or state, which reflects the physical situation of a particular operational environment. These individual models will comprise the overall assessment model.

3.1   Flaw Models

At the start of an assessment, the flaws of the system may or may not be known. As such, the assessor must use the following model to conduct something similar to a high-level flaw hypothesis methodology. As the assessment is conducted, and flaws are identified, the model will be updated.

There are many ways to categorize flaws. In this work, we define flaws in terms of three orthogonal taxonomies: origin, vulnerability to exploitation, and existence of countermeasures.

Flaws (F) exist in both the technical system and in all environments of operations and are defined as:

$$F \text{ represents the set of all flaws} \tag{1}$$

$$F_T \subseteq F \text{ is the set of technical flaws} \tag{2}$$

$$F_O \subseteq F \text{ is the set of operational environment flaw} \tag{3}$$

An operational environment may already contain one or more systems, and as such, is expected to contain technical flaws that are separate, but not necessarily distinct, from a technical flaw of a system being integrated into it. The technical flaws are separate in that they exist on a system that is already part of the operational environment and not the system being integrated into the operational environment, but are not necessarily distinct because both systems could be identical layer 3 switches performing different functions. While the flaws may not necessarily be distinct, the identification and mitigations must be distinct. In this work, it is assumed that all flaws can be designated with an origin that is either technical, environmental (which may contain existing technical flaws considered within the operational environment), or may be designated uncategorized (which includes unknown technical or environmental flaws and will be represented as F_U), and therefore:

$$F = F_T \cup F_O \cup F_U \tag{4}$$

In addition to categorizing flaws by origins, we can further categorize them into exploit classes, specifically those with known exploits (E) and those without known exploits (!E).

To be clear, during the assessment of a system, the technical flaws must always be addressed, because the technical flaws are always part of the system, including when it is implemented into an environment. In addition, the specific operational environment flaws needs to be assessed, categorized appropriately, at the time the system is implemented. Such flaws may expose previously unknown technical flaws, as well as operational environment flaws. Therefore, the set of flaws examined for system s1 will simply be:

$$F_{s1} = F_{O1} \cup F_{T1} \tag{5}$$

However, the above formula indicates flaws are static or unchanging. Therefore, the model requires expansion, by allowing these sets of flaws to be defined dynamically. To model the dynamic nature of the system we define the sets of flaws for a specific system when it is in a particular state. The flaws for a specific state will be those possible flaws given the value of the state variables. We will use the notation $(F_{T1})_n$ to represent the set of technical flaws for system s1 in state n. We will use similar notations for the other sets of flaws.

If $(F_{T1})_n$ and $(F_{O1})_n$ represents the set of technical and operational environment flaws for system s1 in state n, then: the set of all flaws for system1 in state n is:

$$(F_{S1})_n = (F_{T1})_n \cup (F_{O1})_n \tag{6}$$

An assessment of system s1 will then consist of an assessment of the system with respect to flaws in all possible states of the system. If we let $Ev_F (F_{s1})$ represent the assessment of the flaws in system s1 and i represent one of the possible k states, then:

$$Ev_F(F_{s1}) = U_{i=1...k} \, Ev_F \big((F_{s1})_i \big) \tag{7}$$

3.2   Countermeasure Models

Just as flaws exist in a fluid state, so do the countermeasures. This is made more so by the fact that countermeasures are not just on the same system, but exist in more than one layer and in more than one component. Countermeasures are implemented to reduce the vulnerability of an information system.

At the start of an assessment, one would assume the countermeasures of the system should be well identified. Rarely are all of the countermeasures identified at the start of the assessment, primarily due to the complexity of most systems masking some countermeasures and the system owner not always understanding what countermeasures are actually associated with which flaws or vulnerabilities. So, the assessor will not associate the countermeasure model to the flaw model during the initial assessment. Only after flaws and their associated countermeasures are identified, will the two models be correlated.

During the initial assessment, countermeasures will be generically mapped to a flaw area (such as $F_{802.11}$). This allows the assessor to create a high-level representation of the system. This representation will be updated throughout the assessment with the final countermeasure model mapped directly to a flaw model.

Countermeasures (M) may be partial (M_P), complete (M_C), perceived (the countermeasure is in place for a flaw but does not actually mitigate that flaw) (M_{NT}), or not known (M_{NK}). A countermeasure is not known if the countermeasure is possible and applied for this flaw, but not realized as an applied countermeasure. As the assessor's knowledge of the system's flaws and countermeasures increases, the association between the flaws and countermeasures and their associated completeness will solidify.

The set of all possible countermeasures are defined as:

$$M = M_{NK} \cup M_{NT} \cup M_P \cup M_C \tag{8}$$

Countermeasures can be grouped into two categories, those that are complete and all others (M_{NC}). It is assumed that unknown countermeasures are not a subset of complete countermeasures because it is not known if they are complete or not.

$$M_{NC} = M_{NK} \cup M_{NT} \cup M_P \qquad (9)$$

The preceding gives us the categorization of all possible countermeasures. However, for a specific system, we will be examining the subset of countermeasures that are appropriate to that system. The idea is to identify groups of countermeasures that would apply to groups of flaws and then to correlate one or more countermeasures to one or more flaws as the evidence is acquired.

During the assessment of a system, the technical countermeasures must be assessed to determine their affect on the technical flaws, which are always part of the system, including when implemented in an environment. In addition, the specific operational environment countermeasures will need to be assessed and categorized appropriately when the system is implemented to determine their effect on technical and operational environment flaws. The set of countermeasures examined for system s1 will simply be:

$$M_{s1} = M_{O1} \cup M_{T1} \qquad (10)$$

Just as flaws are not static or unchanging, neither are countermeasures. Similarly, sets of countermeasures must be defined dynamically. Just as with flaws, to model the dynamic nature of the system we are going to define the sets of countermeasures for a specific system when it is in a particular state.

The countermeasures for a specific state will be those countermeasures that are possible given the value of the state variables. The notation $(M_{T1})_n$ and $(M_{O1})_n$ will be used to represent the set of countermeasures for system s1 in state n, then a single state of countermeasures for system s1, including the null set, is:

$$(M_{S1})_n = (M_{T1})_n \cup (M_{O1})_n \qquad (11)$$

An assessment of system s1 will then consist of an assessment of the system with respect to flaws and countermeasures in all possible states of the system. If we let Ev (s1) represent the assessment the flaws and countermeasures of the system s1 and i represent one of the possible k states, then:

$$Ev(s1) = U_{i=1...k} \, Ev_F\big((F_{s1})_i\big) \cup U_{i=1...k} \, Ev_M\big((M_{s1})_i\big) \qquad (12)$$

It is not possible to map all of the permutations of flaws and countermeasures [7]. Adversaries are constantly attempting to avoid or overcome countermeasures[7], adding to the fluidity of countermeasures and their associated flaws. The next session provides a mathematical model to be used as a basis for an assessor to document a mapping of a systems flaws and countermeasures.

---

[7] NIST SP800-30 refers to this as threat shifting.

3.3   Vulnerability Models

Vulnerabilities (V) are those flaws that are not completely mitigated by countermeasures. The very high level, conceptual model of vulnerabilities has been defined as:

$$V = F \times M \tag{13}$$

More accurately, vulnerabilities are based on a subset of flaws that are not completely mitigated by countermeasures. Of note, though while possible, it is extraordinarily rare (in fact this author has never witnessed), for a flaw to be completely mitigated in an operationally implemented system. A visually, simplistic representation of vulnerabilities are they are flaws with partial (V_P), perceived (V_{NT}), not known (V_{NK}), or no (V_{NoM}) countermeasures:

$$V = V_{NoM} \cup V_{NK} \cup V_{NT} \cup V_P \tag{14}$$

As vulnerabilities are based upon flaws, in this work we will define vulnerabilities the same as flaws, in terms of three orthogonal taxonomies: origin, vulnerability to exploitation, and levels of existence of countermeasures.

As with countermeasures, vulnerabilities can be grouped into two categories, those that have complete countermeasures and all others (V_{NC}). It is also assumed that vulnerabilities with countermeasures that are not known are not a subset of the vulnerabilities with complete countermeasures because it is not known if they are complete or not:

$$V_{NC} = V_{NoM} \cup V_{NK} \cup V_{NT} \cup V_P \tag{15}$$

As both flaws and countermeasures have fluidity, vulnerabilities have fluidity from constant changing states of both flaws and countermeasures. The vulnerabilities for a specific state will be those flaws and countermeasures that are possible given the value of the state variables. The notation $(V_{T1})_n$ and $(V_{O1})_n$ will be used to represent the set of vulnerabilities for system s1 in state n. Similar notations will be used for the other sets of vulnerabilities. A single state of vulnerabilities for system s1, including the null set, is:

$$(V_{S1})_n = (V_{T1})_n \cup (V_{O1})_n \tag{16}$$

An assessment of system s1 will then consist of an assessment of the system with respect to flaws and countermeasures in all possible states of the system. Just as in the prior section, we let Ev(s1) represent the assessment the flaws and countermeasures of the system s1 and i represent the possible k number of states, then:

$$Ev(s1) = U_{i=1...k} \, Ev_F\big((F_{s1})_i\big) \cup U_{i=1...k} \, Ev_M\big((M_{s1})_i\big) \tag{17}$$

3.4   Threat Models

There are many threat models and no one model will be effective or efficient for everyone. A threat assessment, per CNSSI 4009, is a process of formally evaluating the degree of threat to an information system or enterprise and describing the nature of the threat. Threats are from a variety of sources, such as adversaries, disgruntled insiders, and natural disasters and there are many definitions of cyber threats[8]. A threat, as defined by the NIST Special Publication 800-30 R1, is the potential for a threat-source to exercise (accidentally trigger or intentionally exploit) a specific vulnerability. In this paper, a threat (TR) is some combination of one or more (represented by the superscript +) threat source (TS), that threat source's one or more capabilities (TC), with one or more threat source's motivation(s) (TSM) for exploiting a vulnerability and is defined as:

$$TR = TS^+ \times TC^+ \times TSM^+ \tag{18}$$

Unlike flaws and vulnerabilities, threat sources are defined based upon the intent to exploit. The major categories of intentional human[9] threat sources could be expressed as state sponsored, insider, terrorist, hacker, and organized crime. This is not meant as an all-encompassing list, but enough to provide a basis for an assessor. A threat source, such as state sponsor, is a set because state sponsored not only indicates adversaries in the direct employ of a nation state, but also those that act on behalf of the nation state out of some motivation.

Some would consider that the state sponsored, terrorist, and organized crime to be in the single category of well-funded adversaries, which is the greatest capability. However, the word capability is not sufficiently concise. The initial definition of threat source capabilities is level of expertise, number of resources, and threat source's levels of success.

A threat source has one or more capabilities. A single capability will have one or more resources with each resource having varying levels of expertise and subsequently that capability will have varying degrees of success. A high level example of a threat source of a nation state having multiple capabilities is the USG having the cyber capabilities of the DoD (the individual services) and IC (NSA, etc.). Within this example, each capability has multiple resources (many individual people) each of which will have varying levels of expertise and subsequently the resources, and therefore the capability, will have varying levels of success in attacks.

$$TC = \left(TC_{LevelOfExpertise}\right)^+ \times \left(TC_{Resources}\right)^+ \times \left(TC_{Success}\right)^+ \tag{19}$$

---

[8] CNSSI 4009 defines a threat as any circumstance or event with the potential to adversely impact organizational operations (including mission, functions, image, or reputation), organizational assets, individuals, other organizations, or the Nation through an information system via unauthorized access, destruction, disclosure, modification of information, and/or denial of service.

[9] NIST SP800-30 refers to these as adversarial.

So, a state sponsored threat source may have differing levels of expertise, resources, and success based upon that nation's focus on cyber warfare. Most people assume the greatest level of expertise, resources, and success when considering state sponsored threat sources, but depending upon the situational instance that may not hold true.

The above sets indicate the intentional exploitation or accidental triggering of a vulnerability, as well as the capability of a threat source, but not the motivation. It is often not modeled because there may be no motivation (nature), it may change for each category of threat, and within each threat source based upon situations.

Threat sources, capabilities, and motivations are fluid and change with the situational instance, and at times the technical system. Therefore, the threat states are combination of all possible threat sources, threat source capabilities, and threat source motivations:

$$TR_{States} = TS \times TC \times TSM \tag{20}$$

Just as with flaws, countermeasures, and vulnerabilities, to model the dynamic nature of the system we are going to define the sets of threats for a specific system when it is in a particular state.

The threats for a specific state will be those that are possible given the value of the state variables. The notation $(TR_{s1})_n$ will be used to represent the set of threats for system s1 in state n, then: A single state of threats for system s1, including the null set, is:

$$(TR_{S1})_n = ((TS_{T1})_n \times (TC_{T1})_n \times (TSM_{T1})_n) \cup ((TS_{O1})_n \times (TC_{O1})_n \times (TSM_{O1})_n) \tag{21}$$

An assessment of system s1 will then consist of an assessment of the system with respect to vulnerabilities, and threats in all possible states of the. Just as in the prior sections, we let Ev(s1) represent the assessment of the vulnerabilities and threats of the system s1 and i represent the possible k number of states, then:

$$Ev(s1) = U_{i=1...k} \, Ev_V((V_{s1})_i) \cup U_{i=1...k} \, Ev_{TR}((TR_{s1})_i) \tag{22}$$

Motivation implies some amount of probability[10] of attack occurrence, as does a situational instance, such as a U.S. aircraft in an adversary's airspace during a time of kinetic war. The threat source itself may imply a probability of occurrence, such as a tornado if the system is located in the U.S. state of Kansas, which is highly prone to tornadoes.

3.5   Probability Models

There are three probabilities regarding exploitations to consider during an assessment. There is the probability that a threat source will attack (PA). Then there is the probability of the success of the attack or (PS). Finally, there is the probability of certainty

---

[10] NIST Special Publication 800-30 refers to this as likelihood.

(PC) of the knowledge of the threats, flaws, countermeasures, etc. The overall probability (P) that an attack will occur with some levels of covertness and success would then be defined:

$$P = PA \cup PS \cup PC \qquad (23)$$

To provide the greatest repeatability and reciprocation of the assessment, all three probabilities must be included in calculations. For conciseness, each probability will be individually identified. To be consistent with the NIST Special Publication 800-30 R1, the two of the probabilities in this case will be likelihoods (Almost Certain, Highly Likely, Somewhat Likely, Unlikely, and HighlyUnlikely).

$$PA = \{AlmostCertain, HighlyLikely, SomewhatLikely, Unlikely, HighlyUnlikely\} \qquad (24)$$

$$PS = \{AlmostCertain, HighlyLikely, SomewhatLikely, Unlikely, HighlyUnlikely\} \qquad (25)$$

However, those categories of likelihood do not correlate to the probability of certainty of knowledge. By substituting certain for likelihood, the vocabulary is correct and the values are maintained.

$$PC = \{AlmostCertain, HighlyCertain, SomewhatCertain, Uncertain, HighlyUncertain\} \qquad (26)$$

These probabilities will be defined in terms of their three orthogonal taxonomies: vulnerability countermeasure completeness, origin, and threats knowledge. As with everything else, probabilities exist for both the technical system and in all operational environments. The probabilities can be grouped into two categories, those systems that have vulnerabilities with complete countermeasures and all others.

As well as categorizing probabilities by vulnerability countermeasure completeness, we can categorize probabilities into threat classes, specifically those with known threats and those without known threats. It is assumed that uncategorized threats are a subset of those without known threats.

The technical probabilities can be subdivided into those systems that have vulnerabilities with known exploits and all other technical vulnerabilities. Similarly and generically, operational environment probabilities can be subdivided into those systems that have known exploits and all other operational environment vulnerabilities.

Probability of attack, probability of attack success, and probability of knowledge certainty are fluid and change with the situational instance. Therefore, the probability states are combination of all probabilities of attack, probabilities of attack success, and probabilities of knowledge certainty:

$$P_{States} = PA \times PS \times PC \tag{27}$$

Just as with flaws, countermeasures, vulnerabilities, and threats, to model the dynamic nature of the system we are going to define the sets of probabilities for a specific system when it is in a particular state. The probabilities for a specific state will be those that are possible given the value of the state variables. The notation $(P_{S1})_n$ will be used to represent the set of probabilities for system s1 in state n, then:

$$(P_{S1})_n = ((PA_{T1})_n \cup (PS_{T1})_n \cup (PC_{T1})_n) \cup ((PA_{O1})_n \cup (PS_{O1})_n \cup (PC_{O1})_n) \tag{28}$$

An assessment of system s1 will then consist of an assessment of the system with respect to vulnerabilities, threats, and probabilities in all possible states of the system. Just as in the prior sections, we let Ev(s1) represent the assessment the vulnerabilities, threats, and probabilities of the system s1 and i represent the possible k number of states, then:

$$Ev(s1) = U_{i=1...k} Ev_V((V_{s1})_i) \cup U_{i=1...k} Ev_{TR}((TR_{s1})_i) \cup U_{i=1...k} Ev_P((P_{s1})_i) \tag{29}$$

Probabilities must be considered for both technical and operational environment assessments. However, during the Technical Assessment the probabilities are far from certain. During the operational environment assessment, because the operational environment will have specified threats, there is a greater certainty of knowledge of the probably the threat attack and greater certainty of knowledge of the probably the attack will be successful. No matter the probabilities, without a physical mechanism or vector through or by which the exploit may be conducted against a vulnerability, the exploit won't succeed.

3.6   Attack Vector Models

An attack vector (AV) is a physical mechanism or vector through or by an exploit by a threat source may be conducted against a vulnerability. There are five categories of attack vectors; cyber (AV_{Cyber}), kinetic ($AV_{Kinetic}$), radio frequency (AV_{RF}), supply chain ($AV_{SupplyChain}$), and unknown ($AV_{!Known}$).

$$AV = AV_{Cyber} \cup AV_{Kinetic} \cup AV_{RF} \cup AV_{SupplyChain} \cup AV_{!Known} \tag{30}$$

Attack vectors will be defined in terms of their four orthogonal taxonomies: attack vector origin, attack vector knowledge, multi-vector, and persistence. As with everything else, the attack vectors exist for both the technical system and in all operational environments. The attack vectors can be further grouped into two categories, those attack vectors that are known and all others.

Threat sources must have at least one, but may have multiple attack vectors to facilitate their exploits. As well as categorizing attack vectors by whether an attack vector is known, we can categorize attack vectors into multiplicity classes, specifically those threat sources with multiple attack vectors, those with at least one attack vector, and all others.

It is important to note, that the physical connection between the threat source and the vulnerability must exist only once, and not necessarily be persistent, for the compromise to occur. As well as categorizing attack vectors by multiplicity, we can categorize attack vectors into persistence classes, specifically those threat sources with persistent connection and all others.

Operational environment attack vectors can be subdivided into those systems that have at least one persistent known attack vector and those systems that do not have a known persistent attack vector.

Though not as intuitive an in an operational environment, attack vectors exist for technical systems and can be subdivided into those systems that have a known attack vector and those systems that do not have a known attack vector.

Just as with everything else, attack vectors are not static or unchanging, but fluid and change with the situational instance, and at times the technical system. Therefore, the attack vector states are combination of all possible attack vectors:

$$AV_{States} = AV_{Cyber} \cup AV_{Kinetic} \cup AV_{RF} \cup AV_{SupplyChain} \cup AV_{!Known} \qquad (31)$$

Just as with flaws, countermeasures, vulnerabilities, threats, and probabilities, to model the dynamic nature of the system we are going to define the sets of attack vectors for a specific system when it is in a particular state.

There are two possible states for the attack vectors for that situational instance of a specific system in an operational environment. If $(AV_{T1})_n$ and $(AV_{O1})_n$ represent the set of attack vectors for system s1, in state n, then the set of all attack vectors for system s1 in state n is:

$$(AV_{S1})_n = (AV_{O1})_n \cup (AV_{T1})_n \qquad (32)$$

An assessment of system s1 will then consist of an assessment of the system with respect to vulnerabilities, threats, probabilities, and attack vectors in all possible states of the system. Just as in the prior sections, we let Ev(s1) represent the assessment the vulnerabilities, threats, probabilities, and attack vectors of the system s1 and i represent the possible k number of states, then:

$$Ev(s1) = U_{i=1...k} Ev_V\big((V_{s1})_i\big) \cup U_{i=1...k} Ev_{TR}\big((TR_{s1})_i\big) \cup U_{i=1...k} Ev_P\big((P_{s1})_i\big) \cup U_{i=1...k} Ev_{AV}\big((AV_{s1})_i\big)$$

$$(33)$$

As shown above, not all threat sources would employ every attack vector. Just as not every attack vector would be available to every threat source. An attack vector employed to exploit a satellite would be limited to those threat sources with access to satellites as an example.

3.7   Attack Surface Models

While the term attack surface is more commonly associated with software [7], it is being used more often in reference to operational environments. The attack surface (AS) is all vulnerabilities, both in technical and operational environment that are accessible by attack vectors [8].

$$AS = AV_T \cup V_T \cup V_O \cup AV_O \qquad (34)$$

An assessment of system s1 will now consist of an assessment of the system with respect to threats, probabilities, and attack surfaces in all possible states of the system. Just as in the prior sections, we let Ev(s1) represent the assessment the threats, probabilities, and attack surfaces of the system s1 and i represent the possible k number of states, then:

$$Ev(s1) = U_{i=1...k} Ev_{AS}\big((AS_{s1})_i\big) \cup U_{i=1...k} Ev_{TR}\big((TR_{s1})_i\big) \cup U_{i=1...k} Ev_P\big((P_{s1})_i\big)$$
$$(35)$$

None of the existing assessment methodologies consider attack surface, though Special Publication 800-53A R1 does define attack surface in regards to penetration testing an operational environment. Though the term is becoming more interchangeable with vulnerabilities, it does convey more than vulnerabilities. As such, both terms are appropriate and will be used within this document.

3.8   Impact Models

An impact (I) is the variable result of a threat exercising an attack vector on an attack surface. Normally, impacts are defined in terms of the magnitude of harm, such as in the NIST Special Publication 800-30 R1, using words such as catastrophic, limited, etc. to describe the magnitude. NIST Special Publication 800-30 R1 categorizes harm as damage to operations[11] (I_{OPS}), assets[12] (I_{Assets}), organizations[13] (I_{Org}), and the nation[14] (I_{Nation}). Interestingly enough, loss of human life[15] (I_{Life}) is not included in any of these

---

[11] NIST SP800-30 operational impacts include the inability to perform current and future missions/business functions and damage to image or reputation.

[12] NIST SP800-30 asset impacts include damage to or loss of physical facilities, systems, networks, IT equipment, component supplies and intellectual property.

[13] NIST SP800-30 organizational impacts include harms due to noncompliance, direct financial cost, and damage to reputation.

[14] NIST SP800-30 national impacts include damage to critical infrastructure sector, loss of government continuity of operations, damage to reputation, damage to ability to achieve national objectives, and harm to national security.

[15] Loss of human life is a very real impact not normally indicated in cyber assessments, but when assessing vehicles it would be an operational impact.

categories. Nor is there a category that includes allies[16] (I_{Allies}) or global[17] (I_{Global}) impacts in the NIST Special Publication 800-30 R1 categories. Therefore, impacts will be expanded to include those not considered by NIST Special Publication 800-30 R1.

$$I = I_{\text{OPS}} \cup I_{\text{Assets}} \cup I_{\text{Org}} \cup I_{\text{Nation}} \cup I_{\text{Life}} \cup I_{\text{Allies}} \cup I_{\text{Global}} \qquad (36)$$

The NIST categories of impact contain a mix of both operational and technical impacts. This, again, makes it difficult to separate the technical aspects of a current assessment from an operational environment aspect. To provide clarity, each of the above categories will be further identified to include whether the impact is technical (I_T) or operational (I_O), thus separating technical and operational impacts.

Impacts will be defined in terms of their two orthogonal taxonomies of technical impacts (fail-safe and fail-secure), as well as their two orthogonal taxonomies of operational impacts (loss of life and mission completion).

Fail-Safe references the capabilities of a system to not adversely effect human life or other devices in the event of the system's failure. Fail-Secure is a reference to the capabilities of a system to not allow unauthorized access to data in the event of the system's failure [9].

While fail-safe is a technical taxonomy that involves adverse effect on human life, which may or may not result in loss of life, directly from the system, the operational loss of life impact categorizations are those impacts which result in loss of life in the operational environment and all others.

Regardless of the importance of the mission of a system within an operational environment, impacts are categorized by the ability to complete the intended mission and all others.

As impacts are a direct consequence of a vulnerability being exploited through an attack vector with a certain level of probability of attack and success by a threat source with specific capabilities and motivation, impacts are just fluid and changing at those aspects on which they depend. Just as in other sections, the dynamic nature of they system will be modeled by defining the impacts for a specific system when it is in a particular state.

The preceding example provides a possible state for impacts for that situational instance of a specific system in an operational environment. If $(I_{T1})_n$ and $(I_{O1})_n$ represent the set of impacts for system s1, in state n, then the set of all impacts for system s1 in state n is:

$$(I_{S1})_n = (I_{O1})_n \cup (I_{T1})_n \qquad (37)$$

An assessment of system s1 will then consist of an assessment of the system with respect to threats, probabilities, attack surfaces, and impacts in all possible states of the system. Just as in the prior sections, we let Ev(s1) represent the assessment the threats,

---

[16] Allied impacts include loss of coalition operations, damage to reputation (such as NATO), and damage to ability to achieve coalition objectives.

[17] Global impacts would include the complete failure of the Internet, global-wide virus infection, and global-wide critical infrastructure failure.

probabilities, attack surfaces, and impacts of the system s1 and i represent the possible k number of states, then:

$$Ev(s1) = U_{i=1...k} Ev_{AS}((AS_{s1})_i) \cup U_{i=1...k} Ev_{TR}((TR_{s1})_i) \cup U_{i=1...k} Ev_P((P_{s1})_i) \cup U_{i=1...k} Ev_I((I_{s1})_i)$$

$$(38)$$

Impact models are the last consideration in determining risk. Some would define impact is the probability of risk impacting operations. In some ways, risk is difficult to define because a global impact would imply greater risk, but simultaneously greater risk would greater impact to a system. NIST has the well-accepted definition that impact is a component of risk, and as such it will be followed.

3.9   Risk Models

NIST Special Publication 800-30, Guide for Conducting Risk Assessments[18], defines risk as a function of the likelihood of a given threat-source's exercising a particular potential vulnerability (unmitigated flaw in this dissertation), and the resulting impact[19] of that adverse event on the organization. This definition does not imply any consideration of a situational instance other than a land-based system. Nor does it seem to consider vectors of attack or success of the attack.

To address these considerations, risk (R) is further refined to be the probability of threat source(s) with the capability of exercising an attack vector to exploit a vulnerability for a specific motivation, the probability of success of that attack, the certainty of the knowledge, and the resulting impact(s).[20] Representatively:

$$R = (TS \times TC \times TSM \times PA \times PS \times PC \times AV \times V)^+ \cup I^+ \qquad (39)$$

Simplifying using the attack surface and threat notation:

$$R = (TR \times PA \times AS \times PS \times PC)^+ \cup I^+ \qquad (40)$$

Risk will be defined in the terms of three taxonomies: origin, criticality, and data sensitivity. In NIST documentation, risk is a mix of both operational and technical risks. This, again, makes it difficult to separate the technical aspects of a current assessment from an operational environment aspect. The criticality of the mission, system, and data, are crucial in determining the operational risk associated with a system. Mission

---

[18] Interestingly, it is not the Risk Management Framework (NIST SP800-39) but the Guide for Conducting Risk Assessments which provides the basis for threats, threat sources, and the risk model for the NIST publications, and hence, the USG.

[19] NIST Special Publication 800-39 describes types of adverse impacts at all tiers in the risk management hierarchy.

[20] CNSSI 4009 Defines risk as a measure of the extent to which an entity is threatened by a potential circumstance or event, and typically a function of (1) the adverse impacts that would arise if the circumstance or event occurs; and (2) the likelihood of occurrence.

criticality is the importance of completing the intended mission. Similarly, system criticality is the importance of the system continuing to operate as intended. Whereas, data criticality is the perceived importance of the data residing, transported, or acquired on the system during the mission.

Risk can be further categorized based upon the criticality variables. As values for these variables haven't been defined by the referenced policy documentation, they will be defined as either critical or not critical.

As previously discussed in this proposal, there are multiple methodologies to quantify data sensitivity currently. However, the information, such as classification, may not be known precisely. As such risk will be further categorized only as being sensitive or all others. The technical and operational risk can be subdivided into those with critical data and all other risks.

System level risk is never a single value because there is never just one flaw and countermeasure equating to a single vulnerability, and no one threat or impact to consider. Just as with the aspects previously discussed, risk is not static but fluid. As risk is a set of states, risk is refined to be the probability of a threat source with the capability of exercising an attack vector to exploit a vulnerability of a situational instance at an opportunity in time for a specific motivation, the probability of success of that attack, the certainty of the knowledge, and the resulting impact.[21] Representatively:

$$R_n = (TR \times PA \times AS \times PS \times PC)_n \cup I_n \qquad (41)$$

If $(R_{T1})_n$ and $(R_{O1})_n$ represent the set of risk for system s1, in state n, then the set of all risk for system s1 in state n is:

$$(R_{S1})_n = (R_{O1})_n \cup (R_{T1})_n \qquad (42)$$

An assessment of system s1 will provide the risk for system s1. Just as in the prior sections, we let R(s1) represent the risk the threats, probabilities, attack surfaces, and impacts of the system s1 and i represent the possible k number of states, then:

$$R(s1) = U_{i=1...k} Ev_{AS}((AS_{s1})_i) \cup U_{i=1...k} Ev_{TR}((TR_{s1})_i) \cup U_{i=1...k} Ev_P((P_{s1})_i) \cup U_{i=1...k} Ev_I((I_{s1})_i)$$
$$(43)$$

The dynamic interaction between threats exploiting flaws and defensive entities implementing countermeasures for flaws is constant.[22] This fluidity requires risk not to be a single instance in time decision, but regularly re-assessed. One key decision is how

---

[21] CNSSI 4009 Defines risk as a measure of the extent to which an entity is threatened by a potential circumstance or event, and typically a function of (1) the adverse impacts that would arise if the circumstance or event occurs; and (2) the likelihood of occurrence.

[22] NIST Special Publication 800-30 R1 Defines this as threat shifting, which is the response of adversaries to perceived safeguards and/or countermeasures (i.e., security controls), in which adversaries change some characteristic of their intent/targeting in order to avoid and/or overcome those countermeasures.

often should risk be reconsidered to provide sufficient and accurate determinations.[23] The other key decision in the implementation of any risk decision methodology is determining which security controls are to be assessed during assessments.

In NIST Special Publication 800-30 R1, the Guide to Conducting Risk Assessments, risk is generally assessed and grouped by types of impacts.[24] Based upon the models provided in this dissertation, risk can be assessed and grouped in multiple ways, thus providing increased situational awareness of risk to which one is exposed. NIST Special Publication 800-30 R1 also considers risk for time frames in which impacts are likely to be experience, which is equivalent to situational instances in this paper. This re-enforces the importance of situational instance be considered during operational assessments (especially for vehicles).

4   Moving Forward

The remainder of the research will focus on the new methodology, combining the new methodology into current methodologies, and validating the new methodology in a real world scenario. The first set of tasks will include analyzing the existing, current methodologies:

- Introduce the new methodologies
- Implement the models
- Combine existing and new assessment techniques
- Introduce parallel process methodology

The second set of tasks will focus on the combination of the new methodology into existing methodologies:

- Determine possible points where the new methodologies may be implemented into current methodologies.
- Perform a paper assessment that combines the new methodologies with a current methodology.

The final tasks will be to validate the methodologies and models by:

- Conducting an assessment of a system using these models and methodology while also following existing methodologies.
- Produce a comparison of existing methodologies with and without the introduced methodology.

---

[23] NIST Special Publication 800-30 R1 leaves the length of effectiveness of the results of a risk assessment to the organization to determine.

[24] NIST Special Publiction 800-30 considers risk up through the organization level, which may roll up system levels risks into a single risk at the organization level.

References

1. CNSS, Committee on National Security Systems 4009 IA Glossary, 26 April 2010. http://www.ncix.gov/publications/policy/docs/CNSSI_4009.pdf
2. Chirgwin, R.: http://www.theregister.co.uk/2012/08/02/knight_capital_trading_bug/
3. Markoff, J.: Georgia takes a beating in the cyberwar with Russia. http://www.nytimes.com/2008/08/13/technology/13cyber.html?_r=0
4. Wingfield, B.: http://www.bloomberg.com/news/2012-02-01/cyber-attack-on-u-s-power-grid-seen-leaving-millions-in-dark-for-months.html
5. Johnson, T.: Mathematical modeling of diseases: susceptible-infected-recovered (SIR) model (2009). http://www.morris.umn.edu/academic/math/Ma4901/.../Teri-Johnson-Final.pdf
6. Belik, V., Geisel, T., Brockmann, D.: Recurrent host mobility in spatial epidemics: beyond reaction-diffusion. Eur. Phys. J. B (EPJ B) **84**(4), 579–587 (2011). doi:10.1140/epjb/e2011-20485-2
7. Wikipedia. http://en.wikipedia.org/wiki/Attack_surface
8. Stephenson, P.R., Prueitt, P.S.: Towards a theory of cyber attack mechanics. http://www.ontologystream.com/gFT/Towards%20a%20Theory%20of%20Cyber%20Attack%20Mechanics.PDF
9. Wikipedia. http://en.wikipedia.org/wiki/Fail-safe

Security in Agile Development: Pedagogic Lessons from an Undergraduate Software Engineering Case Study

J. Todd McDonald[✉], Tyler H. Trigg, Clifton E. Roberts, and Blake J. Darden

School of Computing, University of South Alabama, Mobile, AL, USA
jtmcdonald@southalabama.edu,
{tht1002,cer1002,bjd1101}@jagmail.southalabama.edu

Abstract. Integrating agile software methodologies can be fraught with risk for many software development organizations, but the potential rewards in terms of productivity, delivered functionality, and overall success rate are promising. Agile integration may be hard in certain organizational structures, but integrating security into such an approach can pose an even greater challenge. Ultimately, academia must do its part to introduce future computing professionals to these large areas of knowledge. In this paper, we consider the issues and problems of introducing secure agile software principles into undergraduate curriculum. We report observations, results, and pedagogic lessons learned from an empirical study as part of an undergraduate software engineering course. The conclusions and suggestions provide valuable insight for educators and practitioners alike since both communities deal often with how to best introduce agile and security to new initiates.

Keywords: Secure software engineering · Agile · SCRUM · Academic case studies

1 Introduction

Agile methodology emerged at the turn of the century [1] as a software lifecycle paradigm with a general set of principles that promised better productivity and ability to manage change in software development efforts. Over time, applied techniques for implementing agile in team structures have been developed such as Scrum, XP (eXtreme Programming), Kanban, Scrubman, and Agile Unified Process [2, 3]. Proponents of agile believe it has the capability to revolutionize how software is developed because of its focus on stakeholder involvement, test driven development, rapid response to change, and the delivery of incremental working software as a vehicle for feedback [4, 5].

Agile development methodologies have taken the software engineering world by storm in the last decade with a recent survey of over 1000 organizations finding that more companies are "scaling and embracing agile" as part of their software development strategy [6]. According to the VersionOne State of Agile™ results, 94 % of respondent organizations in the USA and Europe practice some form of agile methodology and almost half (45 %) of the respondents worked in development organizations where most teams use an agile approach. Of note, the survey also reports that 47 % of respondents

© Springer International Publishing Switzerland 2016
K. Haltinner et al. (Eds.): CSS 2015, CCIS 589, pp. 127–141, 2016.
DOI: 10.1007/978-3-319-28313-5_9

reported failures in agile project adoption, with 44 % attributing the failure to lack of experience with agile methodologies. As agile is embraced in larger companies and on larger projects, concerns about its viability have been raised [7] to include its focus on delivery over quality, development over planning, and collaboration over management. In the area of quality, security is currently occupying huge media attention and stakeholder interest because of the potential impact of not addressing software vulnerabilities during the development lifecycle. The introduction of security into agile thought is itself a maturing body of knowledge. To address lack of experience and knowledge with agile methods and appropriately highlight secure software principles, the academic world bears responsibility to introduce these concepts into curriculum so that future computing professionals are exposed early and often.

In this paper, we detail our experience with how to introduce secure agile software methods into undergraduate course curriculum and how to best provide a learning laboratory for students. We report observations, ideas, issues, and conclusions from an empirical study centered on a student course project that addressed both secure software engineering and agile methodology. Given potential benefits for agile adoption in corporate environments, the pedagogic issues raised by our experience provide valuable insight for educators and practitioners alike. In Sect. 2, we give a general background on the academic environment of the project, provide an overview of both agile methodology and secure software engineering principles, and mention research work on security with agile. In Sect. 3, we describe the context, parameters, and methodology of the study from a student perspective and delineate the project outcomes. In Sect. 4, we analyze the pedagogic lessons learned and, in Sect. 5, provide suggestions for future related studies.

2 Background

The University of South Alabama (USA), located in Mobile, AL, educates around 15,000 students per year currently. The School of Computing at the USA offers an interdisciplinary program of undergraduate degrees in Computer Science, Information Technology, Information Systems, Health Informatics, and Cyber Assurance. USA and the School of Computing have also received certification as a Center for Academic Excellence in Information Assurance Education/ Cyber Defense by the National Security Agency and Department of Homeland Security. The Computer Science and Cyber Assurance degree programs require students to take two software engineering specific courses: CSC-331 Software Engineering Principles and CSC-440 Secure Software Engineering.

In CSC-331, students are introduced to team-based development, project management, version control and configuration management, unified modeling language (UML), unit testing, artifact management, object-oriented analysis and design, simple design patterns, and iterative/agile lifecycle concepts. The course requires a semester-long course project and student teams are typically 5–6 people in size. Most of the development decisions are constrained completely to include schedule, incremental reviews (spanning two iterations), development environment (Eclipse/Subversion), supporting tools (JUnit framework, Astah UML, Microsoft Project, JavaDoc API), life-cycle (iterative with traditional focus on requirements/analysis/design skills), and plat-form (Android or Java application). The main unconstrained variable is the selection of the project itself: 15–20 choices are provided for students to choose from and teams must self-select their team members, project, and team name. No two teams can have the same topic and School of Computing faculty serve as project stakeholders/customers. Because of typical student time constraints, agile methodologies such as SCRUM are not prescribed for CSC-331 projects because (1) there is a high requirement for stake-holder/customer involvement, and (2) the time periods for in-person or virtual group meetings are limited by diverse student schedules, thus reducing typical software activ-ities to an extended iterative cycle (8–10 weeks versus 2–3 weeks).

In CSC-440, an entire course is devoted to address security in the software lifecycle, which cannot be adequately addressed given the goals of the introductory CSC-331 course which is also the pre-requisite course for CSC-440. The course provides a mixture of knowledge and hands-on experience with secure software engineering (currently structured from the McGraw textbook on secure software [8]) and secure coding (currently supported by the 24 Deadly Sins text [9]). Lab-based assignments cover vulnerabilities such as buffer overflow, SQL injection, cross-site scripting, and race conditions and also cover use of security techniques such as static analysis, penetration testing, abuse case development, and code review. A semester-long project is also required in the course, but with much different parameters than the CSC-331 course project. For CSC-440, course projects are chosen from 20–25 potential idea areas related to secure coding and secure software engineering. Students can work individually or on teams or 2–3 people and are free to choose their topic with instructor approval and guidance. The general goal of the projects is for students to "do" something hands-on by applying the principles, tools, and techniques that are introduced in the course and covered in lectures and labs. One category of project choice is for students to build a piece of software from scratch (their choice of functionality), and show their application of secure software principles as part of the development effort. Students submit a final project technical report and briefing at the end of the course with only a project outline and intermediate midterm report required as incremental deliverables.

A variation of the build-from-scratch category is for students to specifically attempt a software development methodology based on agile techniques and principles. In this case study, we report on the outcomes of a student team that chose this particular form of course project. The student team targeted development of a fully-functional mobile/web application using a customized method for secure agile development. The under-standing, evaluation, and implementation of the study were done through the eyes of students who were still in the process of learning both security and agile principles.

2.1 Agile Methodology

Agile is a fast-paced, iterative lifecycle that places a large emphasis on prototyping and quick delivery. It begins with a conversation with the customer as to what features they want the final product to have, then rates them in order of importance in order to judge which features should be worked on first. These features are then given to the development teams and a time-boxed sprint begins. Agile timelines are made up of a series of short periods of incremental development periods (sprints) and most are short lasting as little as two weeks. During the sprint, each phase of the software development lifecycle (SDLC) is implemented for that feature. In other words, each division of the total project gets its own requirements analysis, coding, testing, etc. along with all of the necessary design documents individually from the other divisions rather than having the project evaluated simultaneously such as in a non-iterative lifecycle like Waterfall. At the end of the sprint, the team should have a finished prototype of the feature they were trying to implement. This marks the beginning of the scrum. The scrum is a meeting between the developers and the customer to discuss possible new features, reorder the current desired features in order of importance, and most importantly, to determine whether the prototype effectively meets the customer's needs. Finally, the development teams are assigned new features to work on and the next sprint begins.

2.2   Secure Software Engineering and Touchpoints

It is no simple task to develop secure software using agile methodology. Since agile is such a fast-paced methodology, in which each phase of the software development life-cycle is implemented into small pieces of functionality created during short "sprints", there is no defined or accepted practice for implementing software security best practices into the lifecycle. From the time agile development came into prominence, researchers have been proposing the correct balance of structure to support security integration through testing, refactoring, and minimal overhead analysis/design [10–12].

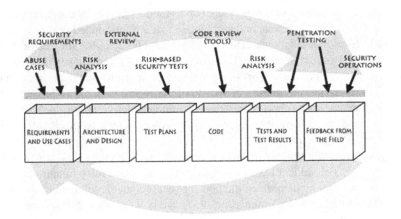

Fig. 1. Touchpoints in the SDLC (Source: McGraw [8], used by permission)

For this project case study, students decided to follow the best practices recom-mended by their course text [8], which McGraw calls "touchpoints". As seen in Fig. 1, each touchpoint correlates to one of the steps of the software development lifecycle (requirements, analysis, design, testing, implementation, maintenance/operations). Touchpoints can be prioritized a posteriori in development prioritized by return on investment, with Code Review (with Tools) and Likewise, each touchpoint comes with its own set of artifacts just like each step of the SDLC. Touchpoints, as described by McGraw, are also "process agnostic", meaning that they should be adaptable to historic sequential methods like waterfall as well as new methods that are iterative. Since agile is an iterative lifecycle, every step of both the SDLC and the touchpoints is applied to each iteration in the sprint before the sprint is evaluated. Thus, each sprint should produce security-related activities and artifacts for whichever piece of functionality is being designed.

3   Case Study Methodology

Students in this particular project began with an introductory knowledge of software engineering and project management skills, experience in programming languages and development tools, and rudimentary knowledge of iterative development practices. For a build-from-scratch project, students had to envision an application functionality, perform standard software engineering lifecycle tasks, integrate secure software principles in development activities, and serve as their own stakeholder for purposes of scope. Agile lifecycles work better when a project can be divided into appropriately small tasks, requiring the students to constrain project vision accordingly. Several other factors influenced the case study project and the selection of the application:

- Small team size (3 members)
- Team members acted as the stakeholder
- Fixed product delivery/functionality deadline (3 months)
- Time estimation required enough time to complete each task from initial requirements to final testing for each piece of functionality
- Project scope had to be significant enough to allow enough material to evaluate where security threats could lie

With these limitations in mind, the students envisioned a mobile application (named *Abject*) that would serve as a scheduling tool for students to enable them to keep track of their classes, grades, and upcoming deadlines. *Abject* required user authentication in the form of user id and password while also storing student information in an online database. Figure 2 shows the basic user interface design targeted for Android devices and the main functionality user interface for adding assignments and classes as well as viewing student grades, assignments, and classes.

3.1   Secure Agile Integration

The student approach to accomplishing the project involved experimenting with how to integrate software security touchpoints [8] into traditional agile timelines. When trying to incorporate this new methodology, the students had to address numerous questions: how often to hold scrums, how long between sprints, and how to keep track of code to name a few. In addition, students had to determine what level of secure software techniques to integrate: what static analysis tools to use, how will testing plans be different, and so forth.

Fig. 2. *Abject* application user interface showing basic functions

Students faced many issues including an initial lack of knowledge with using agile methodology along with proficiency in the languages that were used. Students concluded from their own perspective that very few organizations or groups have documented how to successfully integrate security into the Agile SDLC. Using inspiration from SANS [13], they understand that success required "either constant involvement from security team members or a dedication to security with well-trained coders on every team". Since their team had neither the man-power nor the experience to adequately explore these strategies, they attempted to scale agile activities to support their project timeline within constraints of student life. Figure 3 provides a pictorial overview of the Sprint/Scrum activities that the student team came up with, maximizing independent work activities where possible.

- **Scrum Meetings:** Students originally held scrum meetings once every two weeks, with a Skype meeting every other week. However, not enough work was being accomplished and the team shifted to scrum meetings every Friday. Student schedules in an academic environment do not realistically allow for more frequent scrums.
- **Sprints:** For sprints, students chose a 1 week time period, beginning and ending on Friday. This was primarily due to a small time frame for completing the project and 1 week sprints encouraged constant work on the project. The strategy was to meet often in order to give short-term goals to work on while also fitting into the schedule of a college student who often has other projects to work on with closer deadlines.
- **Stakeholder Involvement:** Since there was no outside customer, students decided for themselves what order to implement features and priority of security issues.

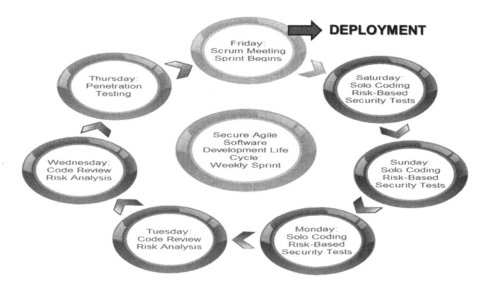

Fig. 3. Student project secure agile schedule

3.2 Software Engineering Activities and Development Environment

The project team accomplished normal software lifecycle activities across sprints including requirements, analysis, design, and testing. The project had numerous requirements due to having two distinct aspects, the application and the development of a secure Agile SDLC. Traditional user and "misuser" stories were developed initially to determine what possible functionality we would need to implement and what vulnerabilities would allow malicious exploitation. Figure 4 illustrates the full use cases derived by the team including user registration, authentication, and user goals for adding assignments, classes, and grades. It also shows the final abuse/misuse case analysis performed as part of secure SDLC across all of the sprints during the course project. The following list delineates other development choices made by the project team.

- **Production/Development Environment:** Since our project is a web application, the team considered several environment including Notepad, Notepad ++, Eclipse, and Aptana Studio, among others. However, thanks to its live preview capabilities and extendibility, the team chose Adobe Brackets to write the application. The team wanted to use Angular because of its pageless capabilities, however, the application did not work correctly outside Bracket's live preview mode and there was no time to find another solution.
- **Source Code Version Control:** The project team used GitHub for source control and version management [14].
- **Testing Environments:** The project team used Brackets' live preview mode for testing the application.
- **Static Analysis:** JSLint was chosen as a static analyzer because it was free and built into the Brackets development environment.

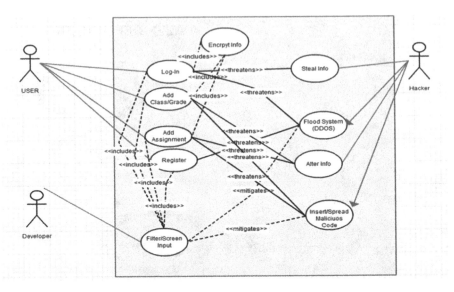

Fig. 4. Abuse/Misuse case analysis

- **Database Tools:** Firebase was chosen as a relational-less cross-platform real-time database [15].
- **Deployment Environments:** The application was originally intended to be multi-platform with support for deployment to W3C-compliant desktop web browsers (Firefox, Chrome, Opera, Safari) and for mobile devices (Android, iOS, Blackberry, Windows Phone 8) through Adobe PhoneGap. Technical issues prevented this full vision and the delivered product could only be deployed via live preview mode from within the Adobe Brackets IDE. Having access to a true hosted web-application server may have solved several issues, but were outside of the scope for a student-led project. The production and test browser supported at project termination was Google Chrome. The *Abject* application was also fed into PhoneGap to produce an .apk for Android, but after producing the original test page, rebuilding did not work and the team did not have time to address this issue.
- **Unit Testing:** Unit testing was intended to be performed before integration testing as the project team completed modules. For example, when a web page was completed, its JavaScript functions would be unit tested. However, the team did not fully complete any of the pages, and never performed a unit test as a result.
- **Integration Testing:** For integration tests, the team adopted the Extreme Programming doctrine of "code a little, test a lot." Code was always in a functional state, even if that state was not entirely secure.

3.3   Example Sprint and Assurance Activities

One of the earliest sprints was for the login functionality. The project team began with normal requirements analysis and developing use and abuse cases, seen in Fig. 4.

Once written, the team considered design and architectural risk analysis. The team desired the application to be multi-platform and to use a "pageless" structure so that when specific buttons were pressed or selections were chosen in a drop-down menu, other contextual menus or options could be added without having to change pages. With these and similar features in mind, the team chose external libraries which had the functions and capabilities required and the team developed a component diagram, seen in Fig. 5. From there, the team analyzed component dependencies for known flaws, vulnerabilities, or exploits which could in turn hurt the system. Later sprints identified data flow diagrams with information boundaries to help assess potential attack points. Mitigation strategies and attack resistance were then considered as part of architectural risk analysis. The team used Microsoft's STRIDE checklist [16] as a guideline to evaluate potential attack patterns.

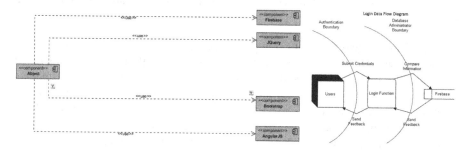

Fig. 5. Component dependencies and boundary analysis for architectural risk

Repeated architectural analysis over several sprints also led to creation of a more full architectural risk analysis which detailed external dependencies, trust levels, entry points, and assets. The STRIDE mitigation strategy was cross-checked against identified threats and potential attack vectors. The project team also performed routine static analysis on developed code samples using JSLint with successful identification of potential vulnerable code and remediation that was scheduled and accomplished in later sprint activities. Code reviews were performed as part of planned sprint activities using friends and colleagues, which focused priorities for work during sprints.

The end-state of the student project resulted in an application with partial functionality and with deployment technical issues still to be resolved. As functionality, initial parts of the register-user feature were completed, allowing a user to input a username and password and be added to the database. The project team spent considerable time with adaptation of security touchpoints within the Agile SDLC.

4 Lessons Learned and Pedagogic Observations

In terms of lessons learned from this empirical case study, the student project team represents a potential sample of developers who are (1) learning agile development techniques for the first time, and (2) learning secure software engineering and programming techniques for the first time. Though their real-world development experience is quite less than most development teams in typical organizations, the education and knowledge insights gleaned from the project team are of interest to all organizations that are actively embracing agile methodologies. As with any drastic organizational change, training and education are keys to success if an initiative is to be viable long term. Our project team faced this and other issues in achieving their goals of integrating security into an agile development lifecycle. We detail these issues and also provide several student learning observations on how to improve both agile SDLC and future academic.

4.1 Impediments to Learning Objectives

The student project team faced challenges and unexpected problems which can be summarized as follows: (1) lack of security knowledge, (2) risk of new technologies and languages, and (3) ambiguity in secure agile situations not normally covered by agile proponents.

Security Knowledge is Critical. A major setback the team experienced was a general lack of knowledge about security before beginning to work on the project. As with many academic settings for teaching and learning software engineering principles, students often "build the boat at sea" by learning techniques over the course of a semester, but yet those same skills are required to be successful in an actual course-long project from the very beginning. According to Microsoft's requirements for secure agile programming [17], each member of the development team must have completed one security course within the last year. However, each member of the student group was learning about security concurrently with developing the product. This approach would work in some lifecycle models, but in agile development, one must cover each of the software security touchpoints in every sprint. Since this project started at the very beginning of the semester, students did not know how to implement the touchpoints in the earlier sprints. In addition, the project team did not know what types of things to look for. For example, in one of the earlier sprints, the students came up with a use case diagram and abuse case diagram for a login screen – one of the first major functionalities that the application needed to have. We considered common attacks such as brute forcing a password or DDOS attacks by creating too many accounts; however, the team had not yet learned about attack patterns such as SQL injection attacks. This is just one example, but throughout development the team would periodically have to go back to reevaluate and remodel the documentation that already created for functionality that should have already been completed because we did not know what to look for as they were designing it. This type of repetition does not follow the agile methodology.

Risks of New Technologies. Another setback faced by the student project was a lack of familiarity with the languages being used to develop the application. The application under development was supposed to be multi-platform, and the team intended to use HTML, CSS, and JavaScript to create the application as if it were a web page, using PhoneGap to convert those pages into a mobile application. The group members had little knowledge of those three languages at the beginning of the project. In an agile lifecycle, each sprint is supposed to add a new functionality, and among adding that functionality, each security touchpoint has to be addressed before the end of the sprint. Our lack of familiarity with the languages we would be using before the project began prevented the team from meeting all of the requirements for the sprint each week and ultimately illustrates the risk of introduced new technologies in a development project.

Problems with Secure Agile in Small Teams. Over the course of the student project, the student team had to consider ambiguous situations that are not always covered by texts or online resources for doing agile methodology. Agile development does not have a defined process for handling bugs, or for that matter, vulnerabilities found in functionality covered in earlier sprints. This is due to the way agile programming works. All of the testing for a particular piece of functionality – for example, the login screen – is performed during the period of the sprint. If all of the work from the sprint has not been completed by the end of the sprint – in our case, one week – then the sprint is elongated and the next sprint is postponed until the first sprint is finished. Due to impediments in knowledge already described, the team had to revisit areas from prior sprints often and had little guidelines on how to do this. Should the current sprint be abandoned in favor of fixing the other issues? Should the team try to fix the other issues while working on the new functionality? The answers to these questions are relatively undefined, at least from the perspective of students trying to find such answers. That being said, agile thought might prefer avoiding such pitfalls and it would therefore be redundant to define what to do when defects are found later on in development. However, the students observed that, even given proper initial training and experience, agile methodologies are not clear on how to handle bugs found in prior sprint delivered functionalities and user stories.

The student project team researched this issue and found a similar problem posted on an agile development blog, Edge of Chaos [18]. In such situations where prior bugs need to be addressed in delivered features, a team proposed that there be an emergency team which handles bugs, vulnerabilities, maintenance, and other small fixes that are found throughout the course of development. The emergency team is chosen by rotation of the features teams. Essentially, they would continue to perform code review and testing even as new sprints continued to develop functionality. While Edge of Chaos did report success with a similar problem, it still posed an issue for the student research project: the main question being whether students can use this version of secure agile to practice software development while learning security. While this idea of an emergency team could be successful in a company with a large number of teams, sufficient manpower, and a longer timeframe, students do not have these same luxuries. It is infeasible to have more than about five people students in a group due to each member having different schedules and other responsibilities. Because of this, the student project team felt that it would not be feasible to construct academic projects with multiple development teams, yet alone an emergency team. The students observed that secure agile in the small scale may not be feasible because security is going to require more time and resources in and of itself.

The end goal of the student project, apart from delivering functional software, was to research the feasibility of creating secure software using the agile software development lifecycle. Due to the setbacks that were encountered, the student project team was not able to reach the best case end goal of having a secure, functional web application. That being said, the student project team did not believe that the project was a failure or that secure development within agile is completely impossible. If the opportunity presented itself again, students on the team felt confident that a similar project replicated by developers who had experience with the programming environment, experience with software security, and an appropriate amount of work hours, the secure agile integration could be a success.

4.2 Student Learning Perspectives

The student project team considered how future pedagogic secure agile projects might be better structured to achieve key learning objectives and enhance student learning. In the original empirical study, the team had a desired end goal of building a piece of secure software by following the agile lifecycle; however, the main problem faced by the team was the need to redo old pieces of documentation to cover vulnerabilities not yet learned, which is a natural consequence of academic environments. The students affirmed strongly that it is impossible to build secure software from the ground up without having knowledge of security before the beginning of the project. Thus, instead of having a singular final goal of "secure software", the student project team proposed a semester-long project centered on the deliverables from the sprints.

The student team proposed a modified set of parameters for future secure agile projects. In the beginning, students in groups of three or four would either choose from a list of possible projects or come up with their own to be approved by the professor. Next, they would design a timeline or schedule for their sprints based on how they decided to divide the project. The dates they chose would become their deadlines for their deliverables. From there, students would follow the secure agile methodology similar to the project team had in mind at the beginning of their empirical study: for each sprint, the team would follow all the steps from requirements to testing, producing all of the required documentation along the way. With their documentation, the students would also provide a few listings from MITRE's Common Attack Pattern and Enumeration and Classification (CAPEC) [19]. The security each team builds in should reflect both the mitigation of the attacks they chose along with any vulnerabilities, weaknesses, or attack patterns that are covered by that time in the course lectures. Once the sprint is over, it is not revisited for further documentation and each sprint's deliverables are graded separately. This allows the students to practice secure software engineering and integrate what they have learned into the project while removing some of the stress of missing something from a previous sprint. At the end of the semester, the final turn-in would be the culmination of all of the artifacts created as an overall design document.

The next logical step from the student team's perspective was to ask how secure agile might work in a production environment. The student's believed their initial experiment demonstrates a proof of concept that secure agile can work in practice, even given their limited initial knowledge and failure to accomplish all of the development they set out to achieve. The students observed that with a larger work force, projects do not have to be divided into such small pieces as in their experiment, so having a large project does not exclude agile as a feasible methodology. They realized that development teams can be broken into smaller feature teams and each feature team can be assigned one of the pieces of functionality to work on. The students believed that designating a rotating feature team which would work solely on bug fixes and other maintenance steps was crucial for ensuring security as a quality software feature.

The students also believed that, even with test-driven development, there is need for a consolidated unit testing cycle before prototypes are delivered to customers and stakeholders for feedback. With many teams working on different parts of the same project, the students realized that it is likely that feature integration will cause emergent bugs not seen by individual feature teams alone. Therefore, they saw the need to run an extra testing phase over the integrated product rather than just the individual functionalities.

Finally, the students concluded that for secure agile to work in practice, regardless of the size of the organization or product under development, every developer and project member should have formal security training to cover both secure software engineering and secure programming, with some training received in the last year, as suggested by Microsoft [17]. The student project team, after having experimented with agile concepts and software touchpoints, concluded that it would not be enough to just have a security team or a security expert on each team to guide the project. After all, building security from the ground up takes time, which creates a conflict of interest between developers who want to develop software quickly.

4.3 Pedagogic Value

Beyond achieving the project specific goals, this student project represents one particular approach at promoting student learning of complex subject matter related to software engineering, security, and agile methodologies. Students had to read material beyond what was offered in the course on their own, research and investigate current thoughts and trends on the subject matter, develop a rationale and approach for how they would integrate these concepts into a tractable project with constrained time and resources, and make course corrections as they acquired new knowledge and ran across roadblocks to meeting their goals. The exercise provided ample opportunity for students to improve critical thinking skills while giving a real-world setting for problem solving skills to be applied. It also reinforced, through practice, the issues of team communication and team workflow management which all real-world projects face. The learning environment allowed for any level of success or failure in evaluating ideas, which the students had to produce on their own, and thus represents a successful model for applied learning as part of an undergraduate curriculum experience.

4.4 Conclusions and Future Work

From a pedagogic viewpoint, our empirical study for teaching and learning secure agile development was largely successful in spite of the project team not meeting all of their expected development goals. Students experienced real-world issues of learning agile from scratch, dealing with imperfect knowledge of security, and balancing technical risk with new technologies. Despite relatively little secure production, working code (which would be a failure in agile thought), the project allowed students to apply what they were learning in course curriculum and ultimately to grow professionally. The students involved also believed secure agile integration could work in practice based on their experience and were even able to come to their own conclusions regarding how best to ensure its success.

From an instructor perspective, we would recommend that any software engineering course focused on agile methodology (typically as an advanced 400 or 500 level software engineering elective), should require a secure software development course as a prerequisite. This would help fill the knowledge gap for secure programming knowledge in the area of vulnerabilities, attack modeling, and remediation. An agile-specific course would also allow an instructor to experiment with a class-based project with delineation of feature teams among the students. Students in such a course should be required to follow secure principles during their normal sprints and as part of their scrum activities, or in whatever agile-specific technique is taught or followed.

For courses that focus on software engineering in general or secure development secondarily, team-base projects focusing on applied agile methods with security should be encourage and promoted. As a necessity, such course projects should be graded primarily based on the attempt of students to apply principles being taught, with an expectation that the amount of delivered/working/secure software is not the primary grading criteria. In the case of CSC-440, we provide students a large degree of freedom to experiment, learn, and even fail as part of their course experience. These lessons learned, particularly when the environment or setting is not perfect, often provide the best opportunity for students to embrace the course curriculum and actually retain knowledge from the course.

Although mandating a class-wide, agile-based course project would not be in line with the overall curriculum goals of CSC-440, we will continue to provide opportunities for students with interest to experiment with using agile techniques while they are learning about integrating security into the software lifecycle. As future work, we will work to constrain the course project based on student recommendations in order to alleviate some of the impediments to success identified by our empirical study.

References

1. Agile Alliance: Manifesto for Agile Software Development (2005). http://www.agilealliance.org/
2. Stellman, A., Greene, J.: Learning Agile: Understanding Scrum, XP, Lean, and Kanban. O'Reilly Media, Inc. (2014). ISBN 978-1449331924
3. Larman, C.: *Chapter 11: Practice Tips* - Agile and Iterative Development: A Manager's Guide (2004). ISBN 978-0-131-11155-4
4. Reliable Software Resources, Inc.: Benefit of Agile Methodology (2014). Accessed 14 August 2015. http://www.rsrit.com/Documents/AgileMethodology_ReliableSoftware.pdf
5. Moran, A.: Managing Agile. Strategy, Implementation, Organisation and People. Springer, Heidelberg (2015). ISBN 978-3-319-16262-1
6. VersionOne Inc: 9th Annual State of Agile Survey (2015). Accessed 14 August 2015. http://stateofagile.versionone.com/
7. Moczar, L.: Why Agile Isn't Working: Bringing Common Sense to Agile Principles. CIO, June 4, 2013 (2013). Accessed 14 August 2015. http://www.cio.com/article/2385322/agile-development/why-agile-isn-t-working--bringing-common-sense-to-agile-principles.html

8. McGraw, G.: Software Security: Building Security In. Addison-Wesley Professional, Boston (2006). ISBN 10: 0321356705
9. Howard, M., LeBlanc, D., Viega, J.: 24 Deadly Sins of Software Security. McGraw Hill/ Osborne, New York (2009). ISBN 10: 0071626751
10. Bartsch, S.: Practitioners' perspectives on security in agile development. In: Proceedings of 2011 Sixth International Conference on Availability, Reliability and Security (ARES), pp. 479–484 (2011). doi:10.1109/ARES.2011.82
11. Siponen, M., Baskerville, R., Kuivalainen, T.: Integrating security into agile development methods. In: Proceedings of 38th Hawaii International Conference on System Sciences (2005)
12. Boström, G., Wäyrynen, J., Bodén, M., Beznosov, K., Kruchten, P.: Extending XP practices to support security requirements engineering. In: Proceedings of International Workshop Software Engineering for Secure Systems (SESS'06) (2006). doi:1-59593-085-X/06/0005
13. SANS Reading Room: Integrating Security into Development, No Pain Required. Accessed 14 August 2015. http://www.sans.org/reading-room/whitepapers/analyst/integrating-security-development-pain-required-35060
14. Github Soure Repository. https://github.com/Jenuma/Abject–Class-Manager
15. Firebase Database. https://www.firebase.com/
16. LeBlanc, D., Howard, M.: Writing Secure Code, 2nd edn. Microsoft Press, Redmond (2002). ISBN 978-0735617223
17. Microsoft Windows Development Center: SDL-Agile Requirements. Accessed 14 August 2015. https://msdn.microsoft.com/en-us/library/windows/desktop/ee790620.aspx
18. Edge of Chaos – Agile Development Blog. http://www.targetprocess.com/blog/
19. MITRE: Common Attack Pattern and Enumeration and Classification. Accessed 15 August 2015. https://capec.mitre.org/

Author Index

Printed in the United States
by Baker & Taylor Publisher Services